OCEAN WASH, POINT CABRILLO SANDSTONE, 1982

SHORELINE, MALPASO, 1962

THE WILDER SHORE

photographs by Morley Baer

text by David Rains Wallace

Foreword by Wallace Stegner

A YOLLA BOLLY PRESS BOOK PUBLISHED BY

Sierra Club Books

SAN FRANCISCO

FIRST EDITION

Photographs ©1984 by Morley Baer. Entire contents copyright 1984
in all countries of the International Copyright Union.

Printed by Dai Nippon Printing Company, Ltd., Tokyo, Japan.

A YOLLA BOLLY PRESS BOOK

The Wilder Shore was produced in association with the publisher
at The Yolla Bolly Press, Covelo, California.
Editorial and design staff: James and Carolyn Robertson,
Dan Hibshman, Diana Fairbanks, Juliana Yoder, and Barbara Youngblood.

The Sierra Club, founded in 1892 by John Muir,
has devoted itself to the study and protection of the earth's scenic
and ecological resources—mountains, wetlands, woodlands, wild shores and rivers, deserts and plains.
Its publications are part of the nonprofit effort
the club carries on as a public trust. There are more than 50 chapters
coast to coast, in Canada, Hawaii, and Alaska.
For information about how you may participate in the club's programs
to enjoy and preserve wilderness and the quality of life,
please address inquiries to Sierra Club,
530 Bush Street, San Francisco, California 94108.

The photographer gratefully acknowledges permission to reprint
photographs that first appeared in his book *Room and Time Enough:
The Land of Mary Austin,* published in 1979 by Northland Press, Flagstaff, Arizona.
Those photographs appear on pages 6, 38, 114, 122, 130, 141.

LIBRARY OF CONGRESS CATALOGING IN PUBLICATION DATA

Baer, Morley.
The wilder shore.

"A Yolla Bolly Press book."
Bibliography: p.
Includes index.
1. American literature—California—History and
criticism. 2. California in literature.
3. Landscape in literature. 4. Literary landmarks—
California. 5. California—Description and travel.
I. Wallace, David Rains, 1945– . II. Title.
PS283.C2B33 1984   810'.9'9794   83-20377
ISBN 0-87156-328-2

ACKNOWLEDGMENTS

I am grateful to William Everson and Lawrence Clark Powell for their writings on California classic literature, which served as a guide and inspiration for my own explorations. Thanks also are due to James and Carolyn Robertson, who suggested the subject of this essay and then kept an open mind when it didn't turn out exactly as they thought it might; to Diana Landau and Dan Hibshman for their interest, encouragement, and useful criticism; and to Barbara Youngblood for her unfailing patience and good humor during the copy-editing process.   D.R.W.

It is sometimes extremely difficult to reach the shoreline in California. The closer the shore to metropolitan congestion, the greater the tension induced by an encirclement of warning signs, barbed wire, and an occasional shotgun. To those owners of land who have watched me in silent forbiddance from their front windows and to others who with a handshake have allowed my trespass, I express a strong sense of appreciation. To those individuals connected by counsel and craft to the actual production of the book—those unseen minds and hands in Tokyo, the staff members of Sierra Club Books in San Francisco—to all of them for their very special abilities, I must express a keenly felt gratitude. My warm thanks go especially to the producers of the book, James and Carolyn Robertson of The Yolla Bolly Press. It was they who first recognized meaning in *The Wilder Shore*. Working as one, as editor and designer, the Robertsons are responsible for pulling together without compromise the diverse photographs into an expressive unit of work. Finally, my profound gratitude goes to one whose activities range from imaginative support in the making of photographs to the most menial job of "spotting" prints, one whose help never fails and whose encouragement cannot be measured, whose force is hidden to most but is evident to me in every photograph, and who first came with me to the wilder shore. To Frances Manney Baer, this group of photographs is gratefully dedicated.
M.B.

CALIFORNIA HEDGE NETTLE AND ICE PLANT, 1967

TABLE OF CONTENTS

CREEKSIDE, GARRAPATA RESERVE, 1982

IN THE 1960s the Sierra Club, until then a publisher mainly of climbers' guides, began to publish books that combined the pictures of great photographers such as Ansel Adams, Eliot Porter, and Philip Hyde and the words of great nature writers, historical and contemporary. The marriage of text and pictures took place as publicly as possible, under intense light, on the highest grades of coated paper, under supervision by some of the world's best printers, often against a background of environmental controversy, and with such success that the Exhibit Format, as it was called, began something of a revolution in publishing.

In *The Wilder Shore* the Exhibit Format, dormant for a good many years, is revived so effectively that one wonders why it was ever allowed to die away. (One knows, of course, but one wonders just the same.) In fact, the photographs of Morley Baer and the text by David Rains Wallace are as firm a marriage as the Club ever arranged, the two elements superbly complementary, each in its way both evocative and explanatory, each focused on the task of bringing California home to Californians.

The book can be viewed, and read, as a gloss on the theme of how a people grows into its living-place. Mary Austin, in *The Land of Little Rain*, enunciated it for the desert: "The manner of the country makes the usage of life there, and the land will not be lived in except in its own fashion. The Shoshones live like their trees, with great spaces between. . . ." And Aldo Leopold, in *A Sand County Almanac*, put it in more general terms: "Wilderness was never homogeneous material. It was very diverse, and the resulting artifacts are very diverse. These differences in the end product are known as cultures. The rich diversity of the world's cultures reflects a corresponding diversity in the wilds that gave them birth."

Nowhere on the continent did Americans find a more diverse nature, a land of more impressive forms and more powerful contrasts, than in California. Nowhere, as both Morley Baer's photographs and Wallace's text make clear, has the land exerted a more profound and multifarious effect on its inhabitants.

Merely looking closely at one of Baer's photographs of the California coast, that "ultimate argument between land and sea," enforces perceptions that are too often half-screened from us by our preoccupations with business or recreation, by our haste, or by our illusions. In the same way, Wallace's admirably objective vignettes, little excursions into the forms and climates and eco-systems of the several regions of California, bring the country powerfully close to us. And Wallace's extended examination of California literature as a response to the landscape stretches the perception backward to 1840, when Richard Henry Dana gave America its first glimpse of California in *Two Years Before the Mast*.

What is at stake in Baer's photographs, in Wallace's impressionistic vignettes, and in the examination of California writers from Dana to London, and from Mary Austin to Steinbeck and Jeffers is the American *response* to California, the response of eager, dazzled, deluded, often misguided, greedy, spiritually impressionable people to country more overwhelming than they had previously known. What is still happening in *The Wilder Shore*, and what Wallace shows us happening in the literature of the past, is the growth of a culture, the slow naturalization of Americans to the California land.

Significantly, the movement of the book is not westward, following the course of empire, but eastward, against the grain of our great expectations. We move away from the shore region, where nature has been at our mercy simply because of the abundance it offers us, and toward the trans-Sierran deserts, where the niggardliness of the land has bent even the Americans toward the adaptation it has enforced on every other species. Every belt of country we pass through provides different pictures, makes different assaults on our perceptions, and has historically resulted in modifications of our way of life and adjustments of our sensibility and our literature.

Critics who live in areas where nature has been completely subdued or was never very impressive in the first place have sometimes complained that California writers make too much of the land and that their writings are too often sentimental celebrations of primitivism. Pondering this book, pictures and text, would persuade even the ghost of Edmund Wilson that in California the land simply cannot be ignored, and never could. From the Pacific shore, "crying out for tragedy," as Jeffers put it, through the mist forests of the coastal canyons into the dry valleys of the Coast Range, where Steinbeck set many of his early stories, across into the great valley, the home of agribusiness from Norris's *The Octopus* to Steinbeck's *The Grapes of Wrath*, and on from there into the Mother Lode foothills, which remember their history as much from the fictions of Bret Harte and Mark Twain as from fact, and still on through the high Sierra that was Muir's province and on finally to the rain-shadow deserts of Mary Austin, this book takes the full measure of California's climates and topographies, and nearly the full measure of its literary production.

Nowhere, I believe, has the study of California writing been made this way, in the very presence of the country that sometimes inspired, sometimes defeated, sometimes appalled the Americans who raided it, exploited it, and have slowly begun to grow into it. The effect is reciprocal. Following Morley Baer's revelation of the state through its complex topography, its belts of climate and microclimate, and its multiple but interlocking ecosystems, we are made more conscious of how important the land has been in the development of a Californian literary sensibility. No matter how we have assaulted and abused it, the land sooner or later imposes itself on us, makes us behave, sets the rules for our existence and therefore for the forms, habits, and arts of our society. And reading the literature and pondering its special qualities, we are made more conscious of how the land has shaped it.

Fortunately, this double effect is available to every reader. As Wallace reminds us, the world is brand new to every individual born into it. We respond to what our own eyes see as well as to what others tell us to see, or tell us they have seen. In that process, literature is both a product and a tool, for "good literature is largely a record of very new and fresh visions of the world, and can be a powerful incentive to seeing, as well as a substitute for it."

Any Californian—indeed, any American—will see better because of this book. It is both an eye-sharpener and a mind-extender, a tool by which we may locate ourselves both in place and in time. It is essential that we do so— the sooner the better. For as Wendell Berry says, "Unless you know *where* you are, you don't know *who* you are."

xiii

TIDAL WASH, GARRAPATA CANYON, 1967

AS HARVARD philosopher George Santayana remarked in 1911, the California landscape makes a strong impression on its inhabitants. It is a strong landscape, a rugged assemblage of sedimentary and igneous rocks recently pushed up from the sea by tectonic movements of the earth's crust, and covered with some of the most striking assemblages of flora and fauna on earth. Santayana said the landscape had become Californians' "spontaneous substitute for articulate art and articulate religion," and this notion has been perpetuated by other eastern observers, not always with the approval that Santayana expressed for nascent West Coast culture. The California brand of nature worship has become associated in many minds with fatuity, with narcissistic Tarzans and Janes on beaches, vegetarians who wear expensive leathers and furs, shamans who drive Mercedeses. Such associations are not unfounded, obviously, but they are oversimplified. If Californians worship their land (and not all do, of course), they don't all do so as mindlessly as some critics seem to think.

California is a very complicated place, as well as a beautiful and rich one. It is full of strong contrasts and quick transitions: in hours one can move from deep forest to glaciated peaks to desert; the vegetation of one valley or mountain may be quite different from that of adjacent ones because of geological or climatic discontinuities. Such a landscape does not really encourage mindless self-absorption. Its sharpness and clarity may dim the preoccupation with human culture that characterizes the urban intellectual, but thought does not concern only human culture, otherwise there would be no human culture to think about.

One cannot know California without thinking pretty hard, because the landscape is so complex and multifarious. In the dry Pacific air, where one can often see hundreds of square miles of forest, meadow, brush, mountaintop,

I

beach, canyon, and valley from a single hilltop, one is impelled to observe, discriminate, draw similarities, speculate—to take up the motions of thought. To venture into this expansive, largely open landscape, it is less necessary to follow established routes than in the flatter, lusher East. Destinations may be visible from miles away, and reaching them can require considerable mental as well as physical exertion.

"What is the nature of that distant patch of chaparral? If I can get through it, I can follow this ridgeline; if not, I will have to climb into the canyon. Does that reddish tinge mean that it is mature chamise brush?" (Chamise flowers turn rusty red when they dry.) "If so, it is probably impenetrable. But if it is mature manzanita, I may be able to crawl through under the almost tree-size plants." Such thinking is a very ancient part of being human. We are here today because our ancestors were good at it.

Of course, complexity is a feature of all natural landscapes, and there are landscapes more complex than the Californian. Still, the steep terrain and brilliant, benign climate of California make complexity harder to ignore than in the low, wooded hills of the East or the rolling grasslands of the Midwest. I lived in the East for twenty-two years without much desire to discriminate between the dozens of deciduous tree species—they were all tall and green and leafy— but when I came to California, I was immediately struck by the contrasts between the rounded oaks, the colorful madrones, the fragrant laurels, and the huge, dark conifers, and I wanted to know more. The California landscape also is harder to push aside into featurelessness than gentler terrain. It is easier, literally, to look down on nature from a New York or Boston high-rise than from a San Francisco or Los Angeles one. Mount Tamalpais and the San Bernardino Mountains won't be looked down on from high-rises.

Santayana was wrong in one respect. California nature worship has been far from inarticulate. California literature is full of articulate thinking about the diverse and exacting landscape. Writers almost always thought about landscape before cities became so big that one could spend one's life in them. The literature of eastern cities may be full of writers whose ignorance of natural landscape is serene, but this is less so in California. Even writers who don't seem to like natural landscape (or don't like writing about it) are impelled to write about wildfires, hillsides, and streams because the state's urban multitudes are so often troubled by droughts, floods, earthquakes, landslides, and other messages from the landscape.

In *The White Album* Joan Didion writes: "It is easy to forget that the only natural force over which we have any control out here is water, and that only recently. In my memory California summers were characterized by the coughing in the pipes that meant the well was dry, and California winters by all-night watches on rivers about to crest, by sandbagging, by dynamite on the levees and flooding on the first floor. Even now the place is not all that hospitable to extensive settlement. As I write a fire has been burning out of control for two weeks in the ranges behind the Big Sur coast. Flash floods last night wiped out all major roads into Imperial County. I noticed this morning a hairline crack in a living-room tile from last week's earthquake, a 4.4 I never felt. In the part of California where I now live aridity is the single most prominent feature of the climate, and I am not pleased to see, this year, cactus spreading wild to the sea. There will be days this winter when the humidity will drop to ten, seven, four. Tumbleweed will blow against my house and the sound of the rattlesnake will be duplicated a hundred times a day by dried bougainvillea drifting in my driveway. The apparent ease of California life is an illusion, and those who believe the illusion real live here in only the most temporary way."

Writers in all parts of the United States have had a deep interest in landscape, of course, but the dramatic aspect of the California landscape has given it a particularly active role in books. It is often a participant in plot and narrative, seldom a passive setting. It seduces characters, then fulfills or betrays them, sometimes kills them. Failure to observe and understand landscape is a mistake that leads to many a tragic ending in California classic literature, and such tragedies have more than incidental significance in a region that has seen a historically unprecedented rapidity of population growth and resource exploitation. The California sun smiles on the immigrant, but there are sharp teeth behind the smile. The Donner Party is a California archetype.

One of the classic ways in which Californians approach an understanding of the landscape is the transect, an ecological exercise whereby one contemplates a cross section of the state, considering geological, climatic, and biotic transitions as one moves, say, from ocean beaches, over coastal mountains, through interior valleys, over foothills and still greater mountains, to the deserts of California's eastern borders. So closely has California literature followed landscape that one can perform this exercise with writers as well as with more venerable fauna. One can transect the state to chart not only changes in the land, but in the way people have felt and expressed themselves about it.

3

CLIFFSIDE NEAR CAYUCOS, 1982

I
The Abundant
Pacific

TIDAL ROCKS, GARRAPATA BEACH, 1969

As I hitchhike north from Eureka in the early morning, the tule marshes along Highway 1 are quite gray with mist and the alder thickets on the cut-over lands are dark. There are berries everywhere: salmonberries, blackberries, salal berries, thimbleberries. A nice place for bears; I wonder if the two words have the same root, bear, berry. I get off at Prairie Creek and follow the trail westward through virgin redwood and Douglas fir forest full of chest-high ferns, which, along with the equally chest-high fallen logs, would make this a very difficult place to walk through if there weren't a trail cut. Yellowish frogs and brown wrens hop in the ferns. Gray, robin-size birds make squawking cries that I at first think are the sounds of distant hikers. The mossy silence here makes sound hard to judge.

Near the ocean, redwoods give way to a newer, thicker growth of spruce and hemlock, with alder groves extending along the creeks into the low, grassy dunes that separate forest from ocean. The creeks don't reach the ocean at this season; they sink into the sand and make bogs. There are elk on the dunes. They fade in and out of the mist, their grayish red coats blending with the vegetation so that they might be mistaken for plants when motionless, especially the bulls with their branching antlers.

There are strong musky smells and scraped places in the sand; the bulls are sparring. Younger bulls lower heads and link antlers and push and pull each other. Older ones merely watch and graze. Farther down the beach a dominant bull has all the cows collected in a herd and occasionally stretches out his neck to bugle.

A sound like radio static comes from the seaward mist, nearly drowning the surf noise. As the day progresses and the mist burns off, I find the sound is made by hundreds of sea birds on the sandbars or floating offshore. There are gulls, pelicans, cormorants, guillemots, sandpipers, terns. There must be schools of fish running; the birds are excited, and the water is full of mammals. Round, earless heads of harbor seals punctuate it regularly, and here and there are small herds of sea lions with longer, sleeker snouts and bull necks. Some kind of large whale spouts on the horizon, and closer in, almost within wading distance at times, pods of pilot whales with square black snouts and small, triangular dorsal fins porpoise through the surf. Sometimes a wave picks up a seal, whale, or fish so that the creature's whole body is visible, suspended in translucent water.

Activity increases as the sun goes down. The gulls spiral high, chasing an osprey that has plucked a large fish from the water. Great blue herons patrol the alder bogs.

7

Three black-tailed deer appear at the edge of the forest. Their red summer coats look electrically brilliant in the warm dusk light, against the bright green alder leaves.

It begins to rain mistily as the sky darkens, but the western horizon holds a nacreous light for a long time despite the clouds. When it finally darkens, the surf starts to flicker and foam with bioluminescence, the bloom of luminous microorganisms, dinoflagellates, that fills coastal waters at this season. The light is so vague it seems unreal, like a nervous disturbance of the retina, but sometimes dark shapes move against it, seal heads or whale backs?

SURF OFF THE SOUTH SHORE, POINT LOBOS, 1962

OCEAN SURF, PESCADERO, 1982

CALIFORNIA is, of course, attached to the rest of America on its eastern border, but America's perception of it really begins with its western edge. It is "the coast" that attracts easterners hungry for a new life, as it has been attracting them since Sir Francis Drake dropped anchor in San Francisco (or Half Moon or Tomales) Bay in the sixteenth century. Long before they knew of its gold or its agricultural potential, California attracted people with the wealth of its Pacific Coast. Even underwater, California is abundant. Upwellings of cold, nutrient-rich water from the Humboldt Current have fostered marine ecosystems of extraordinary value and diversity.

The first place I stayed in California was a little house built on pilings on the east shore of Tomales Bay across from Point Reyes. It was a revelation to me; I had not known a place could be so full of wild animals. Every morning a line of low-flying cormorants seemed to stretch from one end of the bay to the other. The water under the house was alive with long-legged red crabs and orange-fleshed mussels the size of saucers. When I rowed across the bay, herds of sea lions swam alongside and belched their fishy breath at me, and anxious-looking harbor seals seemed to pop up everywhere I looked. I'd seen a harbor seal once before off the Maine coast, and that single seal had seemed pretty exciting, but a little isolated and incidental. But Tomales Bay seemed to belong to the seals as much as to the people. I felt I'd ridden a time machine back to the Pleistocene, when the planet was bursting with big wild mammals. The bay and the grassy hills around it seemed charged with a tremendous potential and excitement.

In the 1830s another young easterner was excited by the California coast's great marine mammal herds. Richard Henry Dana waxed quite enthusiastic about gray whales, and Dana's enthusiasm was not bestowed wantonly upon Mexican California's landscape or people.

MOUTH OF THE LITTLE SUR RIVER, 1969

"This being the spring season, San Pedro, as well as all the other open ports upon the coast, was filled with whales, that had come in to make their annual visit upon soundings. For the first few days that we were here and at Santa Barbara, we watched them with great interest—calling out 'there she blows!' every time we saw the spout of one breaking the surface of the water.... They often 'broke' very near us; and one thick, foggy night, during a dead calm, while I was standing anchor-watch, one of them rose so near, that he struck our cable, and made all surge again. He did not seem to like the encounter much himself, for he sheered off, and spouted at a good distance." (*Two Years Before the Mast*)

Dana's interest in whales probably arose from economic as well as scientific or aesthetic considerations. Whales were the oil deposits of the day, and for Bostonians such as Dana a whale spout must have had implications similar to those of an oil gusher for contemporary Texans. Certainly, Yankee whalers lost no time in exploiting the gray whales, and the great herds Dana saw were a memory by the end of the nineteenth century. The same held true for elephant seals and for sea otters, of which Dana unsentimentally remarked: "The otter are very numerous . . . and being of great value, the government require a heavy sum for a license to hunt them, and lay a high duty upon every one shot or carried out of the country."

If Dana was more concerned with prospects for exploiting California's maritime riches than with the origins or future of those riches, he was simply a man of his time. Wholesale and thoughtless exploitation not only of whales and otters but of every conceivable coastal resource—fish, abalone, crabs, shellfish, gull's eggs, gull's feathers—set the prevailing tone for exploitation farther inland. It also set the tone for the swashbuckling, adventurous variety of California literature, of which Dana was a pioneering and comparatively sober exponent, Robert Louis Stevenson a kind of visiting laureate, and Jack London the apotheosis.

No other California author has been as closely, or as self-consciously, identified with the seafaring life as London. An oyster pirate on San Francisco Bay in his teens, London shipped out on pelagic sealing voyages to Japan and Alaska, and later in life made an epic yacht voyage to the South Seas that nearly killed him. So he wrote with some authority on the ocean frontier; his account of seal hunting in *The Sea Wolf* stands as a type description of the exploitation of California's coastal wealth, even though the novel is set mainly on the high seas.

13

"After a good day's killing I have seen our decks covered with hides and bodies, slippery with fat and blood, the scuppers running red; masts, ropes, and rails spattered with the sanguinary color; and the men, like butchers plying their trade, naked and red of arm and hand, hard at work with ripping and flensing-knives, removing the skins from the pretty sea-creatures they had killed."

For all his love of detailed descriptions of work, Richard Henry Dana could not have written the above scene. Dana saw the California frontier at its beginning, but he was still more observer than participant. Although he took to the sea to escape his genteel Boston origins, it was a temporary vacation. Dana probably witnessed such sanguinary scenes in California, but his essential gentility did not allow him to dwell on them. When he describes a shipboard flogging, it is with an angry detachment that suppresses bloody details.

London, though maturing only at the end of the frontier period, was much more a conscious participant in it, indeed product of it. The distinctly nongenteel elements that comprised the frontier were internalized in London and encapsulated in his seal skinning: pleasure at a rough, outdoor way of life, casual acceptance of violence, an erotic response to intimacy with death ("butchers plying their trade, naked . . . removing the skins from the pretty sea creatures"). Of course, London does not simply glory in the violence and coarseness—he is highly ambiguous about it all—but he participates, with feeling.

It is generally easier to describe things from the outside than from the inside, and *Two Years Before the Mast* is a better book than *The Sea Wolf*. Much of London's writing about the sea, such as *Tales of the Fish Patrol*, is on the level of juvenile magazine fiction. Yet London's writing, because of its ambiguities, has a dimension Dana's lacks. London really *loved* the California coast; this was one of his deepest ambiguities, that he had a delicately sensitive feeling for the wild settings of his he-man dramas. Dana's view of the coast tended toward comfort and convenience: "No thanks, thought I, as we left the hated shores in the distance, for the hours I have walked over your stones, barefooted, with hides on my head;—for the burdens I have carried up your steep, muddy hill;—for the duckings in your surf."

London's tended toward enchantment: "The sudden transition was startling. The moment before we had been leaping through the sunshine, the clear sky above us, the sea breaking and rolling wide to the horizon. . . . And, at once,

LOW-TIDE SURF, CAYUCOS SHORELINE, 1982

as in an instant's leap, the sun was blotted out, there was no sky, even our mastheads were lost to view, and our horizon was such as tear-blinded eyes may see. The gray mist drove by us like rain. Every woollen filament of our garments, every hair of our heads and faces was jewelled with a crystal globule. . . . The mind recoiled from contemplation of a world beyond this wet veil that wrapped us around. This was the world, the universe itself, its bounds so near one felt impelled to reach out both arms and push them back. It was impossible that the rest could be beyond these walls of gray. The rest was a dream, no more than the memory of a dream." (*The Sea Wolf*)

The enchantment is laced with ambiguity; the fog is a smothering threat as well as a source of wonder. The consumptive Robert Louis Stevenson felt a similar ambiguity toward California coastal conditions: "It was to flee these poisonous fogs that I had left the seaboard, and climbed so high among the mountains. And now, behold, here came the fog to besiege me in my chosen altitudes, and yet came so beautifully that my first thought was of welcome." (*The Silverado Squatters*) Stevenson plays with the idea that the fog is the ocean itself, rolling in to deluge the land, and he scrambles up a Napa mountainside to escape it "as the child flees in delighted terror from the creations of his fancy." I remember how quickly squalls could raise the water of Tomales Bay into quite intimidating waves, and the curious mixture of exhilaration and terror I felt when rowing through them.

Enchantment with the coast and ambiguity toward its savagery continued with John Steinbeck and Robinson Jeffers, both residents of the Monterey-Carmel coast that Dana, London, and Stevenson frequented. Steinbeck turned a scientifically oriented eye on the less conspicuous life of the coast, the invertebrate denizens of tide pools, mud flats, and kelp forests. He might not have done so if his friend Ed Ricketts, the marine biologist and author of the classic field guide *Between Pacific Tides*, hadn't guided his vision. Steinbeck was more novelist than naturalist, and the intricate descriptions of marine fauna he embedded in *Cannery Row* glow a little strangely in their amiable, depression-era matrix, like gems in a plum cake, but they are enchanting nonetheless.

"It is a fabulous place: when the tide is in, a wave-churned basin, creamy with foam, whipped by the combers that roll in. . . . But when the tide goes out the little water world becomes quiet and lovely. The sea is very clear and the bottom becomes fantastic with hurrying, fighting, feeding, breeding animals."

Steinbeck saw the analogies between human and animal behavior upon

BEACH AT LITTLE SUR, 1951

which a great deal of modern thought has been based—his tide pools are little microcosms of his dramas of human economic conflict. Jeffers is perhaps modern in a more profound way than Steinbeck, even though he belonged to an earlier generation. Jeffers saw more fully than Steinbeck the implications of the scramble for wealth that the Pacific's abundance had touched off. London and Steinbeck were chiefly concerned that the wealth be divided fairly among men, a venerable and necessary concern of civilization. Jeffers's underlying concern was the more radically scientific one that wealth be divided equally among species and ecosystems—radical in that it did not assume that humanity occupies a qualitatively superior niche from which to manipulate nature with impunity. Jeffers saw in the exploitation of the coast a breaking of ecological balance that could send shock waves to the foundations of civilization.

Jeffers's poems express the mixture of enchantment and ambiguity of the other writers, but then he turns those feelings back on civilization. This is nowhere better expressed than in his poem "The Purse-Seine," wherein a bioluminescent school of sardines caught in a seine at night becomes a metaphor for California's cities:

> How beautiful the scene is, and a little terrible, then, when the
>   crowded fish
> Know they are caught, and wildly beat from one wall to the
>   other of their closing destiny the phosphorescent
> Water to a pool of flame, each beautiful slender body sheeted
>   with flame, like a live rocket
> A comet's tail wake of clear yellow flame; while outside the
>   narrowing
> Floats and cordage of the net great sea-lions come up to watch,
>   sighing in the dark; the vast walls of night
> Stand erect to the stars.
>   Lately I was looking from a night mountain-top
> On a wide city, the colored splendor, galaxies of light: how could
>   I help but recall the seine-net
> Gathering the luminous fish? . . .
> I thought, We have geared the machines and locked all together
>   into interdependence; we have built the great cities; now
> There is no escape.

"The Purse-Seine" is in a way a parody of the frontier viewpoint, which

WINTER TURMOIL, MENDOCINO COAST, 1983

looks upon natural abundance with admiration but with a firm sense that the abundance must be swept away and transformed into human wealth, regrettable though that may be. The poem turns back on civilization the acceptance of violence that allowed the frontier to sweep aside native, wild ecosystems. Jeffers looks upon the civilized abundance of neon-lit cities with admiration but with a firm sense that the abundance must be swept away and transformed into ecological balance, regrettable though that may be. If Jeffers had described London's seal-killing scene in a poem, he might have drawn some simile between the "pretty sea-creatures" London saw flayed on the deck and the pretty women who wear sealskin coats. The uneasy mixture of awe and lust that strikes civilized people during their possession of a virgin country does not go away when the sardines are fished out and the seals decimated. It lingers as unease at the violent implications of that possession.

AFTERNOON STORM OVER POINT SUR, 1971

SANTA ROSA VALLEY NEAR LOMPOC, 1983

II
Coastal Lands: Arcadia and Destiny

MARSH NEAR EUREKA, 1953

The ground is frozen and the grass frosty at sunrise, but the evergreen of madrone, bay, and live oak gives the landscape a subtropical aspect despite the biting wind. The air is very clear, the Farallon Islands starkly visible out to sea. The tide is out in Limantour Estuary; willet and sandpipers tread in the mud. We walk away from the water, over the sweeping headlands, toward the long meadows of Bayview Creek that lead up to the ridge crest.

We pass a group of white-tailed kites on the coastal prairie and coyote bush scrub of the headland, four of them perched on one bush, another on a bush a little farther away. The pattern of white raptors against green shrubs seems to echo a heraldic past, as though we were on some medieval European headland instead of a modern American one. Two ravens fly up from the ground. A dead steer lies in black smears of its own decay, neck stretched out, teeth showing through holes in its cheeks.

Along Bayview Creek the wind lessens, and it is warmer. We see two Indian paintbrushes in blossom, their scarlet bracts as bright red as poinsettia. Wren tits sing in the coastal scrub, and flocks of white-crowned and Savannah sparrows forage along the road. There are little groups of black-tailed deer; I've seen herds of at least thirty here. These little coastal valleys are rich, fog nourished even in summer when the rest of the state is sunstruck. The grass of the old pastures grows over our heads, thick as a canebrake. There are so many meadow mice in the grass that it patters and rustles with their movements. The dirt of the road is covered with predator scats, which are mostly rodent hair and bones. I see bobcats almost every time I come here.

A grove of huge old buckeyes overhangs one segment of the narrow valley. Their gnarled branches and trunks completely bearded over with blue gray Usnea lichen, they look like an oracle grove in some old romance. Deer and cattle have trampled the ground under the trees, I suppose to eat the starchy buckeyes; at least, there aren't any of the nuts left. Ranks of white cumulus clouds stand on the northwest horizon; spider silk and thistledown float past on the breeze. Sometimes everything in this landscape seems to come out of a fairy tale.

It gets chilly again in late afternoon. The sun dips into the western cumulus, leaving a bright red sky and scarlet reflections on bay leaves and pine needles. The wind dies down, and the air pressure seems to change; sounds get clearer. We can hear the alder leaves rustling against one another at every remnant snatch of breeze; we can hear falling leaves popping their stems and settling to the floor of the streamside groves, which are about half-unleaved now. We sit in a grove and listen to a little waterfall and watch leaves shaking against the sky and smell the bittersweet leaf and sap and mold odors. The waterfall is made by an alder trunk that has sunk down and dammed the stream. I wonder how many alder generations lie under our feet in this valley. Alder—elder.

Flocks of quail scuttle between scrub patches; deer come out to graze in the deepening dusk. Cattle low over the hills, almost drowning out a great horned owl that begins hooting farther up the valley. As we climb higher, we pass it. The big bird is sitting on a fence post, gazing straight down as though admiring its reflection in a pool. But there's no pool; it's probably watching a mouse.

GUALALA RIVER, 1983

CLIFFS AT TORREY PINES, 1982

RICHARD HENRY DANA did get pretty excited about the landscape surrounding San Francisco Bay, calling it a "fertile and finely wooded country." In this, he showed a sharp eye for real estate, since California's bay lands, not only San Francisco but Monterey, San Pedro, and San Diego, have proved the most coveted of her landscapes. The Pacific Ocean may be abundant, but we can't live *in* it. On the beaches, headlands, estuaries, and valleys adjacent to it, though, if one doesn't mind a bit of summer fog and winter rain, there is a rare combination of sparkling, maritime air and warm sunny climate that permits a lush, subtropical vegetation without the unhealthy heats and languors of the real tropics. California's coastal lands are, or had the potential of being, about as close to an earthly paradise as nature permits.

Even this benign environment couldn't escape frontier ambiguities, though. The Indians and Mexicans were here first and had to be dispossessed from *their* Eden before the Americans could come into theirs. In *Ramona*, published in 1884, Helen Hunt Jackson gave a glowing picture of the Mexican-Indian Eden of the San Fernando Valley just as it was being appropriated by the Americans: "The almonds had bloomed and the blossoms fallen; the apricots also, and the peaches and pears; on all the orchards of these fruits had come a filmy tint of green, so light it was hardly more than a shadow on the gray. The willows were vivid light green, and the orange groves dark and glossy like laurel. The billowy hills on either side of the valley were covered with verdure and bloom —myriads of low blossoming plants, so close to the earth that their tints lapped and overlapped on each other, and on the green of the grass, as feathers in fine plumage overlap each other and blend into a changeful color. . . .

"Father Salvierderra paused many times to gaze at the beautiful picture. . . .

"It was melancholy to see how, after each of these pauses . . . the old man resumed his slow pace with a long sigh and his eyes cast down. The fairer the beautiful land, the sadder to know it lost."

The natural benignity has its limits, as Joan Didion tells us. The coastal lands have inspired two currents of literary thought, which often run at cross-purposes, but which also mirror one another.

The first current, the more popular, I will call the Arcadian, a word that derives from the name of an ancient Greek pastoral region but which has been extended to describe "any region or scene of simple pleasure and quiet," to quote Webster. Its derivation is appropriate, because the first thing literate Americans did when they arrived in California was liken the coastal lands to the highly poeticized vision of ancient Greece upon which the aesthetic traditions of the genteel East were largely founded. The likeness *is* striking, since California and Greece have similar climates. Nineteenth-century Americans found on the Pacific shore the same mountains clothed with oak, bay, and cedar; the same valleys shaded by palm and cypress; the same limpid, rosy evening light with which they were familiar in the neoclassical canvases of Lorraine and Poussin and in the romantic paintings of the Hudson River school.

Much of the California coastline still resembles a romantic painting. I grew up loving Thomas Cole's "An Evening in Arcady," an extravaganza of sunsets, natural bridges, rosy peaks, piping shepherds, stealthy satyrs, and dancing nymphs, which hung in the Wadsworth Atheneum in Hartford, Connecticut. When I started hiking around Tomales Bay and southward toward the Golden Gate, I sometimes felt like the protagonist in one of those romantic stories about people who step through the walls of picture galleries into living paintings. A landscape at once so grand, with massive stacks of exposed bedrock standing above breathtakingly steep ridges and canyons, and so gentle, with wide grassy swales as soft and green as lawns, did seem extraordinarily romantic to one used to the dense, brushy woods of second-growth New England. I remember one time particularly when I topped a promontory just as the setting sun was reflected in thousands of shiny bay, oak, and madrone leaves so that the top of a little knoll below me was actually bathed in radiance, the light so intense yet mellow as to appear a semiliquid medium. (It's impossible not to use romantic terms such as "promontory" and "bathed in radiance" when describing these things.) A little herd of deer that had been resting on the knoll leapt away in all directions, and I wouldn't have been surprised to see Olympians in tunics and lionskins stalking them.

A young man of classical education, R. H. Dana perhaps felt as I did when he encountered the following scene: "We came to anchor near the mouth of

OLD OYSTER BEDS AT POINT REYES, 1982

DIVISION KNOLL AND BIXBY CREEK, 1982

the bay, under a high and beautifully sloping hill, upon which herds of hundreds and hundreds of red deer, and the stag, with his high, branching antlers, were bounding about, looking at us for a moment, and then starting off, affrighted at the noises which we made for the purpose of seeing the variety of their beautiful attitudes and motions."

Americans were not content just to behold this Arcadian vision. Pragmatic even in imagination, they wanted to *live* it. In the less-populated nineteenth century there was no better place to escape urban corruption than the seashore, where land was cheap and all kinds of seafood were still abundant and free for the taking. The Carmel-Big Sur area, which combined the lush vegetation of northern California with the warmer waters of southern California, became the "Seacoast of Bohemia," a literary Arcadia that began with the colony of San Francisco expatriates led by George Sterling and described by Jack London in *The Valley of the Moon*, and which continued, pushed southward by surging land values, with the artists' colony Henry Miller describes in *Big Sur and the Oranges of Hieronymus Bosch*.

Of course, the simple life was more than a literary phenomenon. It affected, and still affects, every level of Californian (and of American, indeed of Western) civilization. London's and Miller's books have a universal theme: the attempt to escape an urban existence that degraded and corrupted and to find a more independent, peaceful life. Despite major differences of personality and ideology, London and Miller both saw the coast as an arena wherein personal and social liberation might be won.

" 'Oh, I tell you it's just great,' Billy bubbled. 'Look at it for a camping spot. In among the trees there is the prettiest spring you ever saw. An' look at all the good firewood, an' . . .' He gazed about and seaward with eyes that saw what no rush of words could compass. . . . 'An', an', everything. We could live here. Look at the mussels out there. An' I bet we could catch fish.' " (*The Valley of the Moon*)

Might be won. The act of realizing the Arcadian vision soon uncovers a darker current of thought underneath, which I will call the current of destiny. Neither London nor Miller stayed at Big Sur. London took up a lavish but distracted manorial life in Sonoma County, and Miller went back to the big city, Los Angeles. Their destinies did not permit the simple life. They could not break with a civilization that defined them: Miller as its passionate, antic critic; London as its victim, a casualty of alcohol and overwork. Not even a

33

EL SUR RANCHLAND AND POINT SUR, 1963

near-perfect climate and a landscape of surpassing grandeur could keep them where sea birds and trees were their main audience. Miller ends his book by nostalgically dreaming of a thoroughly urbanized Big Sur. "I picture villas dotting the slopes, and colossal stairways curving down to the sea. . . . I see tables spread under brilliant awnings . . . and wine flowing into golden goblets, and over the glitter of gold and purple I hear laughter, laughter like pearling [*sic*] rapids, rising from thousands of jubilant throats."

Miller's urban dream is one of the lapses into sentimentality to which this strange combination of Brooklyn tough guy and Teutonic mystic was occasionally prone. It is like one of those technicolor scenes of alleged classical revelry favored by nineteenth-century academic painters and twentieth-century movie moguls, like a scene from *Ben Hur*. Raymond Chandler provided an unalloyed tough guy's view of the urbanized coast to which Miller fled from Big Sur, a view not without quiet lyricism, but empty of Arcadian delusions. There is plenty of flowing liquor in Chandler's Los Angeles detective novels but little laughter, and certainly none like "pearling rapids." It is not a world where individuals find new lives of personal and social liberation. On the contrary, Chandler's individualist detective fights hard to maintain rudimentary dignity and self-respect in a society of pervasive lawlessness. Liberation has become license.

Covered with roads and expensive houses, Chandler's canyons and valleys remain curiously lonely, in striking contrast to the sunlit, healthful land of chamber of commerce brochures. Chandler's is a landscape of shadows, of mists and exhalations and hidden corruption, of places like the ironically named Purissima Canyon of *Farewell, My Lovely*, where a gigolo blackmailer is beaten to death by a wealthy ex-prostitute.

"There was loneliness and the smell of kelp and the smell of wild sage from the hills. A yellow window hung here and there, all by itself, like the last orange. . . .

"We slid down a broad avenue lined with unfinished electroliers and weed-grown sidewalks. Some realtor's dream had turned into a hangover there. . . .

"Far off the purl of motors, nearer the chirp of crickets, the peculiar, long drawn ee-ee-ee of tree frogs. I didn't think I was going to like those sounds any more."

Escapees from civilization drag their problems with them, either mentally, as with Miller and London, or physically. The basic ambiguity of the frontier

35

is that the pioneer, archetypical simple-lifer, mars the grandeur and abundance he covets by his possession of them. All attempts to return to primal innocence are marred by the frontier's original wound. Destiny hangs on, no matter how the dreamer resists it. Those who resist it less strenuously seem to lead longer lives. London, who persisted in Arcadian ideals, died in his forties. Miller, who sidestepped them, died in his nineties.

Robinson Jeffers positively *embraced* the current of destiny, and he stayed at Big Sur from 1914 until his death in 1962 at age seventy-five. Jeffers looked on the coastal lands much more pessimistically than London or Miller, if even more lovingly, so it does seem a little perverse that he clung to them so much more firmly. Where Miller and London saw in Big Sur the shining promise of a wonderfully bucolic, liberated lifestyle, Jeffers saw it in "Apology for Bad Dreams" as an eternal stage whereon violent destiny met violent apotheosis: "This coast crying out for tragedy like all beautiful places."

Jeffers did not concern himself with the aspirations of bohemians but with the stark lives of the pioneer ranching families who settled the coast. In his narrative poems these epic figures compulsively reenact dramas of violent possession and retribution from which there are no possibilities of escape, only of endurance and transcendence.

> They have done what never was done before. Not as a people
>   takes a land to love it and be fed,
> A little, according to need and love, and again a little; sparing
>   the country tribes, mixing
> Their blood with theirs, their minds with all the rocks and rivers,
>   their flesh with the soil: no, without hunger
> Wasting the world and your own labor, without love possessing . . .
> Oh, as a rich man eats a forest for profit and a field for vanity,
>   so you came west and raped
> The continent and brushed its people to death. Without need,
>   the weak skirmishing hunters, and without mercy.
> Well, God's a scarecrow; no vengeance out of old rags. But
>   there are acts breeding their own reversals
> In their own bellies from the first day.   ("A Redeemer")

Jeffers's vision of the coastal lands is truer than the Arcadian vision's antique, rosy patina. Staying on them so long, he had to see them not in the glamorous

VINEYARDS NEAR ASTI, 1983

SPRING STORM, PORTUGUESE RIDGE, 1971

lights of Arcadian past or future, but in the real, burning, infinitely various sunlight of the living hills:

> . . . fold beyond fold,
> Patches of forest and scarps of rock, high domes of dead gray
>   pasture and gray beds of dry rivers,
> Clear and particular in the burning air, too bright to appear real,
>   to the last range
> The fog from the ocean like a stretched compacted thunder-
>   storm overhung . . .   ("A Redeemer")

In his clarity of vision, Jeffers was a good deal like the real ancient Greeks (he was also classically educated) who inhabited a sunlit, present world where most of life's enjoyment was drawn, not from the amenities of civilization, there being precious few amenities in ancient Greece, but from participation in and contemplation of the natural surroundings. He is also much like the ancient Greeks in his pessimism, for no one knew better than Homer and Aeschylus that nations are raised up in violent possession and cast down the same way.

YOUNG CONIFERS, NORTH COAST, 1962

III
Mist Forests

LEAF LITTER, SAMUEL TAYLOR STATE PARK, 1982

Hitchhiking down Highway 1, we don't get to the trailhead until sunset, but we decide to hike to the nearest campsite anyway. Ceanothus is blooming, and humming-birds are squeaking along the trail; it feels like spring, despite rainy weather. Gray swirls of mist hang on the steep slopes. It's like walking into a Chinese scroll, except that the forest here seems much deeper and darker than that of oriental paintings. The trees and bushes aren't arranged in decorous clumps on picturesque rocky knolls. They smother the mountains with vegetation from the almost black green of redwood galleries along canyon bottoms to the dark shine of oak, bay, tan oak, and madrone on the midslopes to the gray green of chaparral on the ridgetops.

I wonder why oriental landscape painting, indeed landscape painting in general, fails to give a real sense of the depths of forest shade, why trees don't dominate paintings to the extent they do real landscapes. Is it because scholarly or urban painters didn't go far enough into the woods, preferred to look from a safe distance? Or is it because the depths defy pictorial interpretations? It's hard enough to describe them with words.

It gets dark while we're still on the trail, and I find that my flashlight is about to die. It's a steep trail, dangerous in the cloudy dark. Luckily, another party comes along behind us with a good flashlight, so we make it to the campsite, unpack, eat, and go to bed in the dark, being too tired to build a fire. I awaken later, hear a slight noise in the bushes, feel my pack, and find nothing amiss. But the next morning I discover that a raccoon has stolen a pack of noodles and a box of crackers. The empty packages are in the bushes a few feet from my sleeping bag. The raccoon ate it all right there, so deftly that I didn't hear what was happening.

We spend the next day climbing in and out of the Big Sur River canyon, moving eastward toward the crest of the Santa Lucia range. The river is high and cold, hard to ford with a pack. The forest is like that which I'm used to around the Bay Area, but with a few exotic touches, such as the clumps of yucca on sunny ridgetops, reminders that one is getting nearer to the great Southwest. Still, the overall effect at this time of year is of the Northwest, of moisture and mist, deep green moss on the tree boles. Toothworts are in bloom in shady spots, delicate cruciform white flowers minutely veined with purple, the first flowers to bloom in temperate forests across the country.

We spend the night in a redwood grove just below where the range surges up to the

43

narrow, chaparral-covered crest. The great trees follow the canyon bottoms right up to the crest slopes; they look like dark spears thrusting toward the dry flanks of the range. The trees are old and broad but still relatively small compared to those of the north coast, or even of farther west in the Santa Lucias; and the ground under them is poor in the dense greenery that characterizes north coast redwoods, the ferns, mosses, and herbs. The redwoods are facing their limits here but do so in a fittingly tranquil and titanic manner. Their lush foliage seems all the deeper against the dry slopes. The grove is only a few trees broad but nevertheless encompasses a distinct hush, which is easy to sleep in.

We feel energetic the next morning and make it to the crest before noon. The maze of ridges and canyons we crossed coming from the coast seems very short compared to the expanses to the north and south of us. We move along the crest and through a high-country forest of ponderosa pine and Santa Lucia fir; some of the firs, growing on north-facing crags, are still caked with snow and ice from the winter. Then we drop into Pine Valley, a lovely high canyon rimmed with sandstone and floored with meadows and black oak groves. Herds of deer feed in the meadows at twilight, and there is much sign of wild boar on the oak-covered slopes. Years later I meet an old man who tells me he once ate mountain lion meat in Pine Valley.

FERNS AND REDWOOD SPROUTS, NORTH COAST, 1953

ALDERS NEAR LAGUNITAS, 1983

O F COURSE, California is not Greece. Jeffers well knew this:
I am past childhood, I look at this ocean and the fishing
birds, the streaming skerries, the shining water,
The foam-heads, the exultant dawn-light going west,
the pelicans, their huge wings half folded,
plunging like stones.
Whatever it is catches my heart in its hands, whatever it is makes
me shudder with love
And painful joy and the tears prickle . . . the Greeks were not
its inventors. The Greeks were not the inventors . . .

("Hellenistics")

The sunny, oak-dotted coastal grasslands of California give way rather quickly, especially north of Point Conception, to a world unlike anything in Europe, indeed, unlike anything in the ancestral realm of humanity, which goes back only a few million years in depths of evolutionary time which the ancient Greeks would have found inconceivable. A hundred million years ago the redwood forests now scattered along a thin belt of fog-moistened coastal canyons covered most of the Northern Hemisphere—Europe, Asia, Greenland, Alaska, Canada. The dinosaurs lived in them. They not only lived in the redwood forests, they *evolved* in them, grew from sheep-size reptiles to house-size thunder lizards, then suddenly disappeared, leaving the redwoods without herds large enough to graze their needles.

The redwoods seem not to have really accepted the loss of the dinosaurs. In their silence they seem to wait for footsteps unheard these sixty million years. They certainly do little to accommodate the life form dominant at present. Our legs and necks are too short for them. We can't even reach to the tops of the commensal ferns. In the headland and ridgetop oak forests there are acorns, quail, berries, grasses—high energy foods. In the redwoods, mosses, trillium, sorrel, salamanders, a few mushrooms of dubious edibility—little encouragement for the rapacious mammalian metabolism.

47

Literature has responded to the huge, misty coastal forests of California more with dumbfounded admiration than with comprehension or deep affection. Rhapsodists such as Joaquin Miller and John Muir, whom one might have expected to have fastened vociferously on these tallest forests of the world, seem largely to have bypassed them in their odysseys to the more expansive Sierra and Cascades. Perhaps they were a little too shady for someone with Muir's love of light and flowers and clean rock. And even in Muir's time, they were falling fast to a timber industry that had easy coastal access to them. The San Francisco Muir raced through on his way to Yosemite was built of redwood. If he had gone north or south instead of east, he perhaps would have found too many charred stumps for his liking. As he wrote in his unpublished journals: "Had not the Sierra forests grown at a high altitude and thus been rendered difficult of access, they would all have been felled ere this. Meanwhile the redwood of the Coast and the Douglas spruce of Washington and Oregon were more available, though distant. It was cheaper to go up the coast a thousand miles than up the mountains fifty. At Puget Sound, the trees pressed close to the shores as if courting their fate, offering themselves to the axe, while the redwoods filled the river valleys, opening into bays forming good harbors for ships." Tireless defender of wilderness that John Muir was, he was shrewd enough not to make a stand on a rampart already breached.

The coastal writers who lived with the redwoods, if they did not, like Jack London, in *The Valley of the Moon*, view them simply as splendid ornamental pillars for the temple of Arcadia, were vaguely troubled by them. The great trees made a dramatic backdrop for stories, but an overbearing one. John Steinbeck was frankly distrustful of the dark, labyrinthine Santa Lucia Mountains west of his native Salinas Valley, even though he left us one of the loveliest prose descriptions of a redwood canyon in his short story *Flight*.

"Soon the canyon sides became steep and the first giant sentinel redwoods guarded the trail, great round red trunks bearing foliage as green and lacy as ferns. Once Pepé was among the trees, the sun was lost. A perfumed and purple light lay in the pale green of the underbrush. Gooseberry bushes and blackberries and tall ferns . . . met and cut off the sky."

But *Flight* passes quickly from the redwood shadows into the chaparral and oak woodland that Steinbeck liked better, for all their dryness and heat. Steinbeck never looked into the mist forest with the inquiring eye he turned on tide pools and depression waterfronts. If a convivial botanist had laid hands on

MAPLES NEAR CORRALITOS, 1969

EEL RIVER NEAR GARBERVILLE, 1969

Steinbeck the way Ed Ricketts did, it might have been different. Probably not, though. Novelists need action, and though the lives of plants are frenzied enough in the long view, the novel just doesn't run on botanical time, especially not on redwood time. To reverse the Metro-Goldwyn-Mayer motto: Life is long; art short.

Poetry is less obsessed with movement than the novel, and Robinson Jeffers had a particular sympathy for the inanimate:

> The rock walls and the mountain ridges hung forest on forest
> > above our heads, maple and redwood,
> Laurel, oak, madrone, up to the high and slender Santa Lucian
> > firs that stare up the cataracts
> Of slide-rock to the star-color precipices.   ("Oh, Lovely Rock")

Yet it is not so much the quietude of trees as the absolute stability and solidity of rock that Jeffers yearns for:

> . . . Light leaves overhead danced in the fire's
> > breath, tree-trunks were seen: it was the rock wall
> That fascinated my eyes and mind . . .
> Will live and die, our world will go on through its rapid agonies . . .
> > this rock will be here, grave, earnest, not passive: the energies
> That are its atoms will still be bearing the whole mountain above . . .
> > > > ("Oh, Lovely Rock")

If trees are too slow for Steinbeck, they are perhaps a little too fast for Jeffers, a little too soft and flexible. For all their height, redwoods succumb too easily to the leveling, saw-wielding vulgarity Jeffers despised. It is hard to make a symbol of obdurate natural strength out of something that can be so easily turned into a drive-through gas station or a lawn chair. Rock and ocean were more congenial symbols.

Redwoods die, like men, and the forest seems in great part to have been a place of death for Jeffers. The forest is close and dark, it accumulates litter (which Jeffers hated equally with tourism), it lacks the self-cleansing dynamism of surf on headland. Jeffers's heroes and heroines tend to sneak into the shelter of the trees to begin the adulterous, incestuous, necrophiliac, or otherwise devious doings that fuel his tragedies; and he is always meeting moldy old hermits or crazed recluses when he ventures up the canyons.

Amazingly active a toothless old man
Hobbled beside me up the canyon, going to Horse Flats, he said,
To see to some hives of bees. It was clear that he lived alone and
  craved companionship, yet he talked little . . .
    . . . hurried through the shadow-dapple
Of noon in the narrow canyon, his ragged coat-tails flapping like
  mad over the coonskin patch   ("Going to Horse Flats")

Jeffers must have been aware that many people thought of *him* as a crazed recluse moldering in the woods. It is sometimes easier to face the race's destiny than one's own, even if that destiny is consciously chosen, as Jeffers chose isolation. Isolation is easier to bear in some places than others. It is evident from his photographs that Jeffers loved the isolation of open, dynamic places, of windy headlands. But the forest does not permit the expansive reflections of the shore. There is no gazing soulfully with open-necked shirt toward the horizon in the forest. There is no horizon, for one thing, and there are too many mosquitoes and gnats.

The insect clouds that blind our passionate hawks
So that they cannot strike, hardly can fly.   ("Return")

Jeffers spoke often, and very sensibly, of turning the human vision away from the too anxious concern with self that characterizes this overpopulated age, turning it toward the vitality of the inhuman. Yet he was selective about where he turned his gaze. Hawks are not demonstrably less human than flies, but Jeffers certainly preferred them. The nonhuman can be a realm of deterioration as well as vitality, and there evidently were certain eyes that looked back too blankly even for Jeffers's dispassionate gaze. He says he will touch "things and things and no more thoughts," but is fairly fastidious about what he touches: alder leaves and river water, not banana slugs or rattlesnakes.

When he is at his worst, ranting like some rock-ribbed old tory about the superiority of guns and bombers to other modern conveniences, one gets the feeling Jeffers would prefer his audience not to know about his fears. When he is at his best, in poems like "The Deer Lay Down Their Bones," he comes sensitively to terms with the fear of isolation and extinction which wanderers in the sometimes dank and dispiriting coastal forests can feel, with the shadowed, moldy, even dirty side of the other that lives in nature, the other that he invokes more often in the purity of rock, seawater, and hawk's flight.

52

I followed the narrow cliffside trail half way up the mountain
Above the deep river-canyon. There was a little cataract
    crossed the path, flinging itself
Over tree roots and rocks, shaking the jeweled fern-fronds, bright
    bubbling water
Pure from the mountain, but a bad smell came up. Wondering
    at it I clambered down the steep stream
Some forty feet, and found in the midst of bush-oak and laurel,
Hung like a bird's nest on the precipice brink a small hidden
    clearing,
Grass and a shallow pool. But all about there were bones
    lying in the grass, clean bones and stinking bones,
Antlers and bones: I understood that the place was
    a refuge for wounded deer . . .
Here they have water for the awful thirst
And peace to die in. . . .
I wish my bones were with theirs.
But that's a foolish thing to confess, and a little cowardly. We
    know that life
Is on the whole quite equally good and bad, mostly gray neutral,
    and can be endured. . . .
Mine's empty since my love died. . . .
I am growing old, that is the trouble.

With Jeffers's extreme sensitivity to natural phenomena, it's not surprising that he was repelled by the extreme otherness of the mist forest. That otherness has been immediately recognized and appreciated by writers much less attuned to wildness. Henry Miller, a basically urban man despite Arcadian diversions, caught the otherness with wonderful freshness in his overture to *Big Sur and the Oranges of Hieronymus Bosch*:

"In other, olden times there were only phantoms. In the beginning, that is. If there ever was a beginning. . . .

"Who lived here first? Troglodytes perhaps. The Indian came late. Very late. . . .

"Here the redwood made its last stand.

"At dawn its majesty is almost painful to behold. That same prehistoric look. The look of always. Nature smiling at herself in the mirror of eternity. . . .

"Were there once two moons? Why not? . . .

"And what is there to match a faun as it leaps the void? Toward eventime, when nothing speaks, when the mysterious hush descends, envelops all, says all."

Miller was a self-avowed surrealist, and there is a long tradition of fantastical responses to the great old forests, going back to pioneer tall tales, European fairy stories, and Indian myths. A crowd of gnomes, hags, trolls, ape creatures, dragons, nymphs, satyrs, sprites, and spooks still jostles in the unconscious, waiting to be called up as Jeffers's hermits, Miller's troglodytes, Clark Ashton Smith's elder gods, or Steinbeck's dark watchers, the enigmatic, ridgeline figures fearfully glimpsed by the young Indian protagonist of *Flight*.

One of the liveliest evocations of the mist forest's otherness is in Robert Roper's 1977 novel, *On Spider Creek*. In a long monologue by a redwood canyon old-timer, Roper constructs an elaborate, burlesque natural history of the virgin redwood forest before white settlement. It is a forest wherein it rains steadily from October to April, "mudslides and green mold growing up on everything, even on some people's faces," where some trees take "a half an hour just to walk around," where animals that "never saw the light of day in their whole life" prowl. And such animals: blind coyotes with fur like a caterpillar's; giant grizzly bears with human hands and eyes; saber-toothed mountain lions; "enormous herds of perfect little, rat-sized deer stampeding through the woods"; "plus birds and snakes, more snakes and birds than a modern boy such as you could ever dream about. All kinds of weird creatures with double heads and magic poisons in their beaks and feathers and fur mixed up amongst their scales."

What is the purpose of the tall tales? Ostensibly it is to shock, thrill, frighten, but I think there is an underlying purpose that is somewhat the reverse. A backpacking companion once said to me, with a quiet terror: "This place doesn't care at all whether I exist or not."

In a society like ours, which places a premium on *caring*, a perception of indifference in wild nature can be scarier than the idea of being chased through the woods by a hundred screaming demons. The demons may be hostile to one's existence, but at least they show some *interest* in it and thereby affirm it. Furthermore, one can run away from them. The grinning mask of the forest demon can be a way of putting a face on nature, a way of reducing a fear that

FOG IN THE FOREST, POINT ARENA, 1983

BAY, REDWOOD, AND HAZEL, NORTH COAST, 1962

cannot be acted upon to one that can. A hostile forest teeming with weird animals can be conquered or escaped, but what can be done about a forest neither hostile nor friendly, which simply exists? It too significantly suggests that we also may simply exist, that the heavens might look down on *our* fall with no more concern than they do a redwood's. Such bizarre masks can be used to cover the simple, everyday fear Jeffers confesses in "The Deer Lay Down Their Bones," the fear of being alone and mortal in a world one cannot control or even comprehend. By making the forest more fantastic and alien than it actually is, the masks permit us to believe that our lives are altogether different from the apparently isolated, indifferent lives of trees.

OAKS, PACHECO PASS, 1983

IV
Inner Coast Ranges: Sunshine and Poverty

RANCH ROAD, PASO ROBLES, 1976

We camp on the dry grass of a blue oak grove halfway down the side of Coyote Creek canyon. There isn't enough water to cook with, so we eat a dry supper and then climb to a muddy, algae-choked old cattle pond to see if any animals come to drink in the dusk. Earlier we saw mountain lion tracks in the dirt of the road.

The sun takes a long time to set, its light staying on the other side of the canyon until the ridgetop glows red against the darkening eastern sky. Something about that sky seems to hint at the presence of the San Joaquin Valley on the other side of the ridge; there's a feeling of concavity, of denser air. Perhaps it's just that I know the valley is there, that the land east of the ridge is almost treeless, though the canyon is green with oaks.

Acorn woodpeckers cackle and scrub jays squawk inquisitively. Tree swallows skim over the cattle pond to drink, then bats replace them as light fades. A little humidity rises from the pond, and the smell of tarweeds gets stronger. The yellow- or white-flowered tarweeds are about the only living herbs in the grass now, they and the creeping, gray-leaved turkey mulleins. The wild oats, fescues, and filarees that made the hills green a month ago are rattling beige skeletons. Resins in the tarweeds allow them to stay a sulfurous green all summer. My tennis shoes are yellow and sticky from walking through them.

No animals appear, and it becomes very dark; there's no moon. The dry air doesn't retain the sun's heat; it turns chilly, so we walk back down the slope and get into our sleeping bags. Despite the chill, the air still smells of dust. The stars are not particularly bright overhead, despite the solitude here. Too much dust in the air, I suppose.

The chill drains away quickly the next morning as the sun warms the air. The first rays to reach us in the grove are already hot, making skin feel greasy and prickly. Flies and cicadas start to buzz energetically. California ground squirrels make high-pitched alarm sounds that have a metallic ring to them and carry far in the still air. The silvery beige squirrels have blackish patches on their shoulders, as though they've been scorched or tarred, aesthetically appropriate markings for this sunburnt landscape, but biologically puzzling. The squirrels' overall pale beige color makes them inconspicuous and cool in the hot grassland; black patches would seem to have an opposite effect, to make them conspicuous and hot by attracting hawks and absorbing sunlight. The squirrels are so common, however, that such a harmful effect seems unlikely. Maybe the black patches cut down on glare, as with the black grease spots football players smear under their eyes. A hawk's eye might be caught more by a glint of sunlight on silvery beige than by a black patch.

We climb to the canyon bottom to escape the heat, which is giving me a headache. It's narrow and stony, but there's evidence of past habitation: a treeless patch, perhaps a field or pasture once, and a rickety building that may still be in use as a hunting camp. There are mattresses and a stove inside. The creek is running feebly, stony trickles between sandy pools. Big sedge tussocks growing in the moisture look invitingly green to walk through, but I part them with a stick before stepping, and soon find a medium-size, beige and gray rattlesnake that has taken refuge in their shade. Rattlesnakes don't like getting sunbaked any more than we do, particularly since they can't control their body temperature by sweating or other warm-blooded means. The snake is calm and departs without any show of hostility.

The minnows that live in the creek pools are much more aggressive. When we sit in the pools to cool off, they attack us vigorously, although their jaws are too weak to break the skin, even to cause pain, and only tickle rather pleasantly. I suppose they're feeding on the dead cells from our sunburnt hides. They're welcome to them; this must be a hard place for a fish to live.

PINES AND CHAPARRAL, FIGUEROA MOUNTAIN ROAD, 1982

HILLSIDE PASTURE, CLOVERDALE, 1983

IF THERE IS such a thing as a forgotten land on the bustling West Coast, it is the tangle of oak and pine woodlands, grassland, and chaparral that covers the ridges and valleys just east of the coastal mist forest. It is a land where if one asks an old man how the place has changed in fifty years, he will probably tell you that there are fewer people now. It is a land that was covered with tiny towns and schoolhouses and homesteads at the turn of the century, but where one can now walk for three days, as I have, and see bobcats and coyotes and golden eagles and many falling-down houses still full of the furniture and antique utensils of families who abandoned them half a century ago, but no people, except perhaps a cowboy in a jeep.

If one takes such a walk in winter or spring, one may wonder at the solitude. Why did people leave this green, smiling land of tall grass and rushing streams? If one walks in the summer, one knows why. The grass is dead, and the streams are dry, and what had seemed an earthly paradise in April seems precisely the opposite in August. There is too little water in the hills for the subsistence farming and small ranching that the homesteaders of eighty years ago tried to do.

Steinbeck's story *Flight* is a study in the California Coast Range sun's power to wrest water, and thus life, from an unwary humanity. Steinbeck's young fugitive is doomed almost as much by the loss of his water bag as by the posse that pursues him.

"In the grey light he struggled up the last slope of the ridge and crawled over and lay down behind a line of rocks. Below him lay a deep canyon exactly like the last, waterless and desolate. There was no flat, no oak trees, not even heavy brush in the bottom of it. And on the other side a sharp ridge stood up, thinly brushed with starving sage, littered with broken granite. Strewn over the hill there were giant outcroppings, and on the top the granite teeth stood out against the sky.

"The new day was light now. The flame of the sun came over the ridge and fell on Pepé where he lay on the ground. . . . His eyes had retreated back into his head. Between his lips the tip of his black tongue showed."

Homesteaders who tried to settle such country left the sad history of their enterprises on the maps. A ragged strip of Poverty Flats, Poor Man's Valleys, Dry Creeks, and other discouraging words runs from Redding south to Bakersfield. They don't seem to have left much else in the way of written records. The experience was not a colorful one, like the gold rush. It was the standard nineteenth-century story of pioneer settlement, except that in this case it failed, and failed largely during the drought of the 1920s, a time when poverty was even less fashionable than it is now. It was not until the depression had elevated poverty that the story of the inner coast ranges' small, drought-ridden farmers was told by John Steinbeck in *To a God Unknown* and *East of Eden*.

To a God Unknown is a strange novel that has justly been called "prose Jeffers." Its complex, symbolic theme—a drought-maddened homesteader immolates himself, opening his own veins as an act of sympathetic magic to bring back the rains—is like those of Jeffers's narrative poems, as is its pantheist lyricism. The novel is rapturous in its landscape descriptions: there was a poet in the younger Steinbeck that evidently faded in the older novelist. The frightening contrast between the smiling, rain-nourished face of the hills and the savage, drought-stricken one is nowhere better evoked than in passages at the beginning and end of the book.

As the hero arrives to take up his homestead: "Joseph gained the ridge-top and looked down on the grass lands of his new homestead where the wild oats moved in silver waves under a little wind, where the patches of blue lupins lay like shadows in a clear lucent night, and the poppies on the side hills were broad rays of sun. He drew up to look at the long grassy meadows in which clumps of live oaks stood like perpetual senates ruling over the land. . . . 'This is mine,' he said simply, and his eyes sparkled with tears and his brain was filled with wonder that this should be his. . . ."

As he prepares to abandon it: "He rode slowly home along the banks of the dead river. The dusty trees, ragged from the sun's flaying, cast very little shade on the ground. . . . The hills were gaunt now; here was a colony from the southern desert come to try out the land for a future spreading of the desert's empire. . . .

". . . He passed a dead cow with pitifully barred sides, and with a stomach

RANCHLAND, BIG SUR, 1969

swelled to bursting with the gas of putrefaction. Joseph pulled his hat down and bent his head so that he might not see the picked carcass of the land."

Steinbeck's prose tragedy doesn't work as well as Jeffers's verse ones, partly because the kind of poetic dialogue it entails sounds peculiar in a novel, partly because Steinbeck doesn't embrace the current of destiny as uncompromisingly as Jeffers does. It is always clear in Jeffers that tragedy results from hubris, from refusal to pay attention and respect to the limits that an indifferent physical world places upon human pride and appetite. Steinbeck is aware of destiny—his characters are destroyed as thoroughly as any in Jeffers—but he seems to have trouble keeping his eyes on it. A kind of folksy, Arcadian sweetness keeps creeping in. Steinbeck's homesteader never seems to suspect that, by putting four families, a large livestock herd, vegetable gardens, grain fields, and other improvements on a square mile of hilly oak woodland, he might be doing something at best foolish and at worst arrogant. He is aware that *something* is wrong, but it is something outside his grasp, something cosmic and portentous. By this, Steinbeck probably meant him to seem mythic and heroic, but he merely seems dense. So the ending, when he opens his veins to bring back the rain, seems more Hollywood bittersweet than tragic catharsis, because tragedy requires that its protagonist learn something from his predicament, and Steinbeck's is more or less let off the hook. His sacrifice is a success, the rains come back, and the innocent Mission Indians dance happily in the mud.

Steinbeck's hero somehow thinks he is *helping* the land by running as much livestock as he can on it, and the death of grass and livestock still doesn't convince him that the land might have a life of its own, which people can only use or "enhance" within strict limits. Unlike his hero, Steinbeck knew that land could be loved to death. His description of what the Oklahoma farmers of *The Grapes of Wrath* did to their land demonstrates this. But he seems unwilling to express the implications of this knowledge. Perhaps he thought tacit irony was enough, but I doubt it. From the ending of *To a God Unknown*, one might imagine that the hero's brother (who had fled with the remaining cattle, sensibly) would return to the homestead and take up again the life of the soil. But history is sometimes truer than fiction. The valley Steinbeck set the novel in is now part military reservation, part nature preserve. The drought-stricken Coast Range was not "a colony of the southern desert"; it was a place with its own cycles of life, which the patriarchal hero did not trouble to understand before setting out to people it.

68

EEL RIVER, DOS RIOS, 1983

RANCHLAND NEAR SAN LUIS OBISPO, 1982

Perhaps Steinbeck could not let his hero see the stupidity of his enterprise because the hero was a poor man, and Steinbeck was sentimental about poverty. Steinbeck had an eloquent hatred of injustice, but anyone reading *Tortilla Flat* or *Cannery Row*, or even *The Grapes of Wrath*, gets a sense that poverty is rather a purifying and ennobling thing. And if poverty is so, then things that perpetuate it, such as misuse of natural resources or runaway population growth, cannot be a deep source of anger or concern, as long as poor people are doing them. For rich people to do them is another matter, of course. A world without poverty would have been unpleasant for Steinbeck because he didn't like well-to-do people. In *East of Eden* the rich lettuce farmers of the Salinas Valley suffer the pangs of destiny, while the poor homesteaders of the hills are comforted by many children and Arcadian joys.

Steinbeck might not have been able to admire poverty if California had been a *really* poor place. Most of the homesteaders had already left the hills when he came to write *To a God Unknown*, voting with their feet for urban paychecks over Arcadian austerities, so his lyrical approach to the subject benefited from a certain historical detachment. If the homesteaders had stayed in the hills, their landscape might have become more suitable for description by Faulkner, Ignazio Silone, or other chroniclers of truly bitter and ingrained rural poverty. But they didn't, sensibly, and today a hiker not averse to climbing a few fences (most of the area is now in large ranches or corporate hands) can still experience something of what Steinbeck's hero did in discovering the hills: "As he rode, Joseph became timid and yet eager, as a young man is who slips out to a rendezvous with a wise and beautiful woman. . . . The endless green halls and aisles and alcoves seemed to have meanings as obscure and promising as the symbols of an ancient religion."

SAN JOAQUIN VALLEY NEAR MANTECA, 1983

V
The Great Valleys: Arcadia Mechanized

FARMHOUSE, MONTEZUMA HILLS, 1983

SAN LUIS ISLAND, MERCED COUNTY
APRIL 1983

The San Joaquin River is a sheet of brown water, inundating fences and willow thickets, stretching toward the southern horizon. Oaks, cottonwoods, and buttonbushes stand in it. The margin of the flood is strewn with little freshwater clamshells, their mother-of-pearl insides a pretty blue violet color. Two of the shells lie on top of a sawed-off tree trunk, where a raccoon evidently climbed to eat them. Mallards and coots sail among the willows, happy that their river world has expanded. A black-crowned night heron flaps away from the shore with a croak as I approach.

A beaver suddenly surfaces among the willows, only a few feet from where I sit. It swims out of sight, apparently not noticing me. When I stand up a little later, there is a loud slap and splash as it dives. I expect to not see it again, knowing the shyness of beavers, but to my surprise it quickly resurfaces and climbs out on a little platform of twigs under a willow and crouches there as though watching me. I idly throw some bark chips into the water near it, and it surprises me again by swimming out as though to investigate them. I wonder if picnickers have been feeding it. When I leave, it is still crouching on the platform. I'm surprised to have seen it at all; I thought beavers had become quite rare in the San Joaquin.

I spend the afternoon walking southward through an almost uninterrupted green grassland. There's nothing but grass, sky, and a few clumps of iodine bush before me, no orchards, plowed fields, grain elevators, utility lines, or other artifacts of valley civilization. On the west is the Coast Range; on the east, the river's willows and cottonwoods; on the north, the dilapidated shack headquarters of Kesterson National Wildlife Refuge, with a flock of swallows billowing around it. The cliff swallows have built their mud nests under its eaves so thickly that I'd be afraid they would pull the roof off. Clouds are piled up against the Sierra, but I get a few glimpses of white peaks (or what look like white peaks; it's hard to tell them from cumulus clouds at this distance) before the gray slant of rain cuts them off. Then shreds of rainbow hover fitfully over the gray curtain, as though to remind one that there is something beautiful behind it.

A patch of blue catches my eye in the grass. I turn and find a vernal pool in full bloom beside the road. The cracking mud bottom of the recently dried pool is covered with Downingia, *heavenly blue flowers (marked with yellow and white) characteristic of vernal pools. They share the mud with a bewildering variety of exotic-looking, bright green plants—a plantainlike grass; a big, spiky plant not yet in bloom; tiny*

75

mosslike quillworts; and pillworts and liverworts. Around the pool's edge is a yellow ring of goldfields, a miniature sunflower relative, mixed with white popcorn flower and yellow owl's clover.

The expanse of grass is dotted with pools. Some are quite large, and one of these, also recently dried, is completely overgrown with goldfields. It looks as though a patch of earth has taken fire and grown molten. A ground squirrel hops across an edge of this pool, carrying its tail up over its back—another surprise. The California ground squirrels I'm used to don't do that. This is an antelope ground squirrel, a species characteristic of deserts that also lives in the San Joaquin Valley.

Many pools still hold water, and waterfowl—black-necked stilts and avocets and yellowlegs, pintails and shovelers and cinnamon teal. The stilts make a great racket as they teeter about on their improbably long, bright red legs. These long-lasting pools are alkaline sinks, rimmed with white deposits of crystallized salts and smelling like the home permanents my sister and her friends used to give each other when they were teenagers. The salt in the soil here is the main reason why this grassland still stretches into the distance. Little earthen mounds beside the sinks are thick with annual grasses and riddled with burrows—of squirrels, kangaroo rats, badgers, foxes, coyotes. Meadowlarks, redwings, horned larks, and Savannah sparrows fly up at almost every step through the grass. Pheasants squawk, killdeers and nighthawks roost on pebbly spots, a burrowing owl flaps away low to the ground, pursued by dive-bombing blackbirds. Interspersed with the ammonia smell of the sinks are breezes of intoxicating freshness and fragrance, the breath of a million wild plants.

SPRING PLANTING NEAR GUINDA, 1983

SUTTER BUTTES NEAR MARYSVILLE, 1977

T HE HISTORY of the San Joaquin, Sacramento, and other large, alluvial valleys of California's interior is somewhat the opposite of that of the inner coast ranges. While the hills presented an apparently Edenic environment that proved hostile to dense settlement, the great valleys seemed hostile at first—arid or marshy, infernal in summer and dank in winter, flat, malarial—but proved agriculturally bountiful beyond the wildest expectations of the pioneers. Water was available in the valleys: it could be drawn unfailingly from the gravelly ground or the mountains; it did not depend on the winter rains. When the hero's brother in *To a God Unknown* resolves to save his cattle, he drives them to the only permanent pasture available, along the San Joaquin River a hundred miles from the hill homestead.

Where the natural landscape of the Coast Range is largely intact, that of the valleys is largely gone. A level expanse of bunch grass prairie, tule marsh, vernal pools, alkali scrub, valley oak savannah, and riparian forest (tangles of huge oaks, sycamores, cottonwoods, ashes, walnuts, vines, and herbage that John Muir likened to jungle), valley landscape was easy to push aside, and has been pushed aside so enthusiastically that state and private nature preservation organizations are scrambling frantically to save a few examples of each type before it disappears from its four-hundred-mile-long by fifty-mile-wide habitat.

John Muir was struck with the beauty of the still-natural San Joaquin Valley when he arrived in California in the spring of 1869. His description of his first sight of it, and of the mountains beyond, is an archetype of California landscape appreciation.

"The grandest and most telling of California landscapes is outspread before you. At your feet lies the great Central Valley glowing golden in the sunshine, extending north and south farther than the eye can reach, one smooth, flowery, lake-like bed of fertile soil. . . .

79

"When I first enjoyed this superb view, one glowing April day, from the summit of the Pacheco Pass, the Central Valley, but little trampled or plowed as yet, was one furred, rich sheet of golden compositiae, and the luminous wall of the mountains shone in all its glory. Then it seemed to me the Sierra should be called not the Nevada, or Snowy Range, but the Range of Light."

(*The Mountains of California*)

Muir's ethereal vision of the Central Valley is gone as completely as the California grizzly. Today, from the valley, the Sierra usually looks like a range of dust, a vague swelling in a petrochemical haze. All that glitters on the valley floor is not golden wildflowers but car windows, transmission towers, and irrigation equipment (there is the occasional field of yellow mustard, an alien weed). There are still a few places that echo a primevally spectacular ecosystem, such as the federal wildlife refuges where improbably large flocks of snow geese billow like sparkling confetti on the horizon, or the state and private preserves where native wildflowers still bloom in orderly succession around vernal pools and riparian forest still shades the streams. But one must travel far and look closely to find them.

Not surprisingly, the ephemeral beauties of the great valleys have not bulked large in California literature. Most writers have dwelt, and still dwell, on the valley's negative side—heat, flatness, chilly tule fogs, monotony. There is a feedback cycle in this. The less people appreciate the valleys, the less worthy of appreciation they become as their native ecosystems are plowed and bulldozed away. They become nonplaces, interchangeable with the rest of agroindustrial America, a land of enormous, irrigated fields, concrete culverts, and endless, flat, herbicided roads, with only a freeway gas station sign to relieve the monotony of the horizon. When smog obscures the mountains, as it often does, the valleys might as well be Illinois or Kansas.

The California valley is not Kansas or Illinois, though. Stolid and midwestern as it may seem in its welter of feed lots, tomato fields, and strip developments, it, too, partakes of the tension between dreams of Arcadia and misgivings of destiny that have made the West Coast so attractive and repulsive to the rest of America. The Arcadia the valley offers, and the destiny, are not as poetic as those of Jeffers's, or even Steinbeck's, coast, but they are more substantial. The valley soils are deep and stable and rich. The dream of small, self-sufficient family farms that has been America's dream since Jefferson is

SAN JOAQUIN RIVER IN FLOOD NEAR LODI, 1983

SLOUGH OF THE SACRAMENTO RIVER NEAR ISLETON, 1983

possible in the California valley as it is not in the Coast Range. It is a dream that successive waves of farmer-immigrants have had as they looked down from the surrounding mountain passes. Steinbeck expressed their feelings in *The Grapes of Wrath*.

"They drove through Tehachapi in the morning glow, and the sun came up behind them, and then—suddenly they saw the great valley below them. Al jammed on the brake and stopped in the middle of the road, and: 'Jesus Christ! Look!' he said. The vineyards, the orchards, the great, flat valley, green and beautiful, the trees set in rows, and the farmhouses."

With its mild climate, plentiful water, and rich soil, the California valley might have been a real mass Arcadia for Steinbeck's dust-bowl refugees or London's downtrodden factory workers, a land of many small, flowery villages equal to the carefully domesticated landscapes of the Old World.

But the American destiny of violent possession and retribution could not be escaped in the valley any more than on the coast. When something was really worth grabbing, Americans didn't stop at grabbing it from Indians and Mexicans, they grabbed it from one another. So the early settlers who wrested the valley from tule elk and grizzlies found it wrested from them in turn by railroads and trusts. Frank Norris's *The Octopus* is an epic of such land grabs, based on a historical event, the Mussel Shoals Massacre of the 1880s. It does not tell the meager story of a few homesteaders destroyed by drought, but the big one of rich wheat ranchers farming thousands of acres who are nonetheless bankrupted, driven from their lands, and virtually executed by the railroad companies that control the shipping of their produce to market.

Published at the turn of the century, *The Octopus* shows how very quickly the valley's natural landscape was pushed aside. Except for a few shade trees and willow arroyos and some sheep-pasture hills, there is no natural habitat in the thousands of acres Norris describes.

"All about him the country was flat. In all directions he could see for miles. . . . Nothing but stubble remained on the ground. With the one exception of the live-oak by Hooven's place, there was nothing green in sight. The wheat stubble was of a dirty yellow; the ground parched, cracked, and dry, of a cheerless brown. By the roadside the dust lay thick and grey, and, on either hand, stretching on toward the horizon, losing itself in a mere smudge in the distance, ran the illimitable parallels of the wire fence. And that was all; that and the burnt-out blue of the sky and the steady shimmer of the heat."

The only wild animals in *The Octopus* are hordes of jackrabbits the ranchers round up and slaughter for an afternoon's entertainment. The only flowers are the artificially grown ones of a commercial seed farm.

The valley of *The Octopus* is an industrialization of the Arcadian American dream. It is not a land domesticated for human habitation: it is a land scraped bare for machines, where thirty-five giant plows work a field at once. Norris makes this plain in the thoughts of a rancher's wife: "She remembered the days of her young girlhood passed on a farm in eastern Ohio—five hundred acres, neatly partitioned into the water lot, the cow pasture, the corn lot, the barley field, and wheat farm; cosey, comfortable, home-like; where the farmers loved their land, caressing it, coaxing it, nourishing it as though it were a thing almost conscious; where the seed was sown by hand, and a single two-horse plough was sufficient for the entire farm; where the scythe sufficed to cut the harvest and the grain was thrashed with flails.

"But this new order of things—a ranch bounded only by the horizons, where, as far as one could see, to the north, to the east, to the south and to the west, was all one holding, a principality ruled with iron and steam, bullied into a yield of three hundred and fifty thousand bushels, where even when the land was resting, unploughed, unharrowed, and unsown, the wheat came up— troubled her, and even at times filled her with an indefinable terror. To her mind there was something inordinate about it all; something almost unnatural. The direct brutality of ten thousand acres of wheat, nothing but wheat as far as the eye could see, stunned her a little."

About her husband, the wheat farmer Magnus, Norris has this to say: "At the very bottom, when all was said and done, Magnus remained the Forty-niner. . . . It was in this frame of mind that Magnus and the multitude of other ranchers of whom he was a type, farmed their ranches. They had no love for their land. They were not attached to the soil. They worked their ranches as a quarter of a century before they had worked their mines. To husband the re-sources of their marvellous San Joaquin, they considered niggardly, petty, Hebraic. To get all there was out of the land, to squeeze it dry, to exhaust it, seemed their policy. When, at last, the land worn out, would refuse to yield, they would invest their money in something else; by then, they would all have made their fortunes."

Magnus and his wife seem modern in their attitudes, even though we may assume neither had ever ridden in an automobile. The conflict between the

SPROUTING MILLET IN THE SACRAMENTO VALLEY, 1983

BARN AT DUNNIGAN, 1983

small Arcadian model of farming and the big industrial one continues and is as full of ironies as it was when ruthless, mechanized Magnus was being swallowed alive by the even more ruthless, mechanized railroads. Steinbeck reported on its progress in the 1930s in *The Grapes of Wrath.*

"The little farmers watched debt creep up on them like the tide. They sprayed the trees and sold no crop, they pruned and grafted and could not pick the crop....

"This little orchard will be a part of a great holding next year, for the debt will have choked the owner.

"This vineyard will belong to the bank. Only the great owners can survive, for they own the canneries, too."

The artificialized landscape of the California valley is really two landscapes, the small owner's and the big owner's. The small owner's is an Arcadian crazy quilt of little gardens, orchards, vineyards, pastures, and crop fields. In *The Octopus* it is represented only by the seed company garden and an old Mission garden, but it is a little more prevalent than that. It is the landscape inhabited by William Saroyan's ebullient Armenians, sought by Steinbeck's Okies, and admired by Aldous Huxley and other intellectual simple-lifers. Lacking the glamour of the coast, it is probably more durable in its Arcadian aspirations because of its abundant earthiness. The blazing sun and flatness that make the undomesticated valley seem desolate are better for growing things than the poetic coastal breezes and mists, as long as there is water. Unlike Jeffers's brooding ranchers, its inhabitants are voluble, gregarious, and hopeful. No amount of mortality and calamity seems capable of subduing Steinbeck's Joads, as long as they aren't actually starving or fleeing the law.

But the valley's wealth is guarded jealously from the Joads: "The truck moved along the beautiful roads, past orchards where the peaches were beginning to colour, past vineyards with the clusters pale and green, under lines of walnut trees whose branches spread half across the road. At each entrance-gate Al slowed; and at each gate there was a sign: 'No help wanted. No trespassing.'"

The small owner's landscape is a scattered, localized one, clustering at the edges of towns, where jobs are available. Small-scale subsistence farming does not lend itself to the acquisition of consumer conveniences. Even the small owner's farming is mechanized today, with Rototillers, pickups, chainsaws, and whatnot, none of which can be acquired without cash. The landscape of big ownership stretches all around the small holdings, a sea in which the waves are arranged in orderly, dirt brown rows.

As Joan Didion tells us in *Slouching Towards Bethlehem*: "The landscape . . . never, to the untrained eye, varies. The Valley eye can discern the point where miles of cotton seedlings fade into miles of tomato seedlings, or where the great corporation ranches—Kern County Land, what is left of DiGiorgio—give way to private operations . . . but such distinctions are in the long view irrelevant."

Like a sea, as Steinbeck observed, it has a way of eroding the small, leafy islands of Arcadia. It is not a populous landscape, the big owner's, occupied largely by Mexican field hands and the occasional, palm-decked mansion. According to Norris and Steinbeck, it is not a very hopeful one. This may seem paradoxical: Why should people who have so much be pessimists? Perhaps their view is merely sentimental. Still, the big owners in books like *The Octopus* and *East of Eden* do seem so beset by the anxieties of holding on to their empires, so threatened on all sides by pests, weeds, weather, labor, the stock market, and politics as to not get much pleasure out of life. The brooding sense of isolation and insecurity in Steinbeck's Salinas Valley lettuce growers is in strong contrast to the sunny heedlessness of his bums and Okies. Given Steinbeck's genteel origins, there may be more truth in the brooding than the sunniness. It's harder to sentimentalize a group you belong to.

"All day long, all that moves is the sun, and the big Rainbird sprinklers. . . .

"It is when you remember the Valley's wealth that the monochromatic flatness . . . takes on a curious meaning, suggests a habit of mind some would consider perverse. . . . An implacable insularity . . ." (*Slouching Towards Bethlehem*)

Despite the optimism of small owners, one does not get much confidence from Norris and Steinbeck that they will inherit the valleys. Norris was ambivalent about the small-big conflict because he admired bigness, was impressed with the mammoth, inhuman scale of mass agriculture. He keeps breaking out in rhapsodic passages about "The Wheat! The Wheat!" and describes at great length how it flows out of the combines, into the freight cars, onto the ships that will "feed the world." Steinbeck foresees an agrarian revolution in *The Grapes of Wrath*, but his potential revolutionaries were absorbed by the wartime industrial economy, an economy that did much to solidify the pattern of mass agriculture.

RICE FIELDS NEAR KNIGHT'S LANDING, 1983

SYCAMORE NEAR AMADOR CITY, 1983

VI
The Mother Lode: Treasure and Horror

STANISLAUS RIVER SHALLOWS BELOW SONORA, 1983

The valley grasslands are already dry and yellow, but inside the red rock walls of the canyon, the vegetation is vernal, the ash and oak leaves a tender green, the syca-mores just barely leafing out. The wildflowers are colorful but delicate, as though needing the canyon's shelter: pink, twining snake lily; tufted, pale violet pussy's ears; white and gold iris. Songbirds glow against the new foliage: scarlet and yellow of western tanager, gold and black of northern oriole, turquoise and cinnamon of lazuli bunting, indigo and orange of cliff swallow.

Butte Creek shakes and roars with its burden of snowmelt. Overhanging trees drip with spray. The water is too cold to swim in. It crashes over the big granite boulders as though it meant to erode them away in a couple of days instead of hundreds or thousands of years, as though geological time were more impatient here than in other places. The steep gradient from Sierra snowpack to valley floor seems a natural sluice. Flecks of quartz glitter like gold in the granite, and in the sand at the bottom of apple green pools.

The canyon bottom is pitted and gullied, evidence of placer mining, I suppose. Sleeping on a clifftop above the creek I have strange dreams. I stand on a dry, brushy mountainside at night and see a glow of orange light coming from around a rocky shoulder. I walk along a path and come upon primitive mines dug cavelike into the mountain. Miners work with picks and shovels in the lamplight. They are grotesque, like Goya clowns and witches. I wonder why they work at night, why they leave their homes and families to troop up the mountainside in the dark. There is a meaning implied, something rather ghastly: a dead past come to life, or unable to rest. Their clothes are gray and moldy-looking.

The next day we follow the canyon eastward along the overhanging buttes. The floor is a narrow line of verdure far below, insignificant in the foothills' jumble of sunburned rock, dead grass, chaparral, and digger pine. The spring wildflowers remaining up here blossom at the ends of wiry, desiccated stems that are almost invisible in the sun's glare, so that the red or yellow flowers seem to hover in thin air, buoyed by the heat. The songbirds are drab: towhees, wren tits, bush tits. This is a land of kangaroo rats and tarantulas. Someone told me of driving around here at night

93

when there were so many kangaroo rats bouncing across the road that it was impossible not to run over them.

Farther east the canyon slopes up to gentle highland valleys. The grass in the long pastures is still green and short, and the black oaks along them are just coming into leaf, a mist of violet and pale green against dark pines and firs. Dogwoods are flowering in the shade. Creeks meander boggily through the pastures, only occasionally exposing the granite and glittering quartz that the water will erode so violently downstream.

THE FOOTHILLS of the Sierra Nevada and related Klamath Mountains are an object lesson in the power of geology over history. Ecologically, they are almost identical to the inner coast ranges: rising out of the central valleys first in broad, grassy swells, then in hills bearing oak, madrone, and digger pine, then in steep, chaparral-covered ridges, finally in dissected plateaus of ponderosa pine, incense cedar, and white fir. But the ultramafic and igneous rocks of Sierra and Klamaths are much older than the Coast Range's sedimentary and metamorphic rocks. They contain treasures from the earth's mantle, as though elder, chthonic demons have been at work in them, storing up temptations for the planet's human inheritors. As tectonic stresses have cracked and uplifted these ancient rocks during the past two million years, rivers have washed millions of tons of gold-bearing quartz from them and deposited the gold in their canyons.

So the Mother Lode's history has been much busier, not to mention bloodier, than the inner coast ranges'. The Sierra foothills are as green and flowery in spring as their transvalley counterparts, and they have attracted their share of ranchers and homesteaders, but this trickle of Arcadia seekers was inundated almost from the beginning by a flood of treasure hunters whose attitude toward land, inhabitants, flora, and fauna was essentially that of an invading army. There has never been much of an Arcadian vision attached to the Mother Lode, at least, not until the real estate boom of the 1960s and 70s, when just about anything not yet under asphalt was hopefully seen as an investment in bucolic bliss. True, there were sentimental lithographs and paintings showing ruddy-cheeked miners reposing in leafy bowers on their Sundays off. But the miners themselves did not view the foothills with much sentiment. To them, the Mother Lode was a place to go through quickly—get in, get rich, get out. Most of them got out without getting rich, which did not lighten their view of the landscape. One of these unfortunates, an indolent Missourian who called himself Mark Twain, described the countryside in a way that probably was approved by most of his compatriots.

"All scenery in California requires *distance* to give it its highest charm. The mountains are imposing in their sublimity and their majesty of form and altitude, from any point of view—but one must have distance to soften their ruggedness and enrich their tintings; a Californian forest is best at a little distance, for there is a sad poverty of variety in species, the trees being chiefly of one monotonous family—redwood, pine, spruce, fir—and so, at a near view there is a wearisome sameness of attitude in their rigid arms, stretched downward and outward in one continued and reiterated appeal to all men to 'sh!—don't say a word!—you might disturb somebody!' Close at hand, too, there is a reliefless and relentless smell of pitch and turpentine; there is a ceaseless melancholy in their sighing and complaining foliage; one walks over a soundless carpet of beaten yellow bark and dead spines of the foliage till he feels like a wandering spirit bereft of a footfall; he tires of the endless tufts of needles and yearns for substantial, shapely leaves; he looks for moss and grass to loll upon, and finds none, for where there is no bark there is naked clay and dirt, enemies to pensive musing and clean apparel. Often a grassy plain in California is what it should be, but often, too, it is best contemplated at a distance, because although its grass blades are tall, they stand up vindictively straight and self-sufficient, and are unsociably wide-apart, with uncomely spots of barren sand between." (*Roughing It*)

This passage is as much a description of its author's state of mind as it is of the landscape. It is a state of mind one might expect in a young man engaged in a hazardous, arduous enterprise thousands of miles from home; a state of mind common in armies—jauntiness and rough jocosity, buttressed by male camaraderie, and overlying a deep well of loneliness and sadness.

"But they were rough in those times! They fairly reveled in gold, whisky, fights and fandangoes, and were unspeakably happy. . . .

"It was a driving, vigorous, restless population in those days. It was a *curious* population. . . . For, observe, it was an assemblage of two hundred thousand *young* men—not simpering, dainty, kid-gloved weaklings, but stalwart, muscular, dauntless young braves, brimful of push and energy, and royally endowed with every attribute that goes to make up a peerless and magnificent manhood—the very pick and choice of the world's glorious ones. . . . the strangest population, the finest population, the most gallant host that ever trooped down the startled solitudes of an unpeopled land. And where are they now? Scattered to the ends of the earth—or prematurely aged and decrepit—

MALAKOFF DIGGINGS, 1983

or shot or stabbed in street affrays—or dead of disappointed hopes and broken hearts—all gone, or nearly all—victims devoted upon the altar of the golden calf—the noblest holocaust that ever wafted its sacrificial incense heavenward. It is pitiful to think upon." (*Roughing It*)

It's no wonder Twain found a close look at the California landscape depressing. A close look at anything to do with the gold rush must have been depressing. There were bodies buried everywhere, both literally and figuratively, bodies first of Indians and Mexicans, then of murdered miners, lynched miners, diseased miners, suicidal miners. The gold rush was a frontier with a vengeance, on the southwestern model, with the extra impetus that a hot climate gives to rampageousness.

Mark Twain was of course a humorist, but he was not a sunny-natured or optimistic man. Humor for him was not a bright core of reality but a shiny wrapping that covered not only sadness and loneliness but a necrophiliac fascination with violence, death, and corpses. Thus his "humorous" accounts of everyday mining town events such as this: "We were introduced to several citizens . . . among others, to a Mr. Harris, who was on horseback; he began to say something, but interrupted himself with the remark:

" 'I'll have to get you to excuse me for a minute; yonder is the witness that swore I helped to rob the California coach—a piece of impertinent intermeddling, sir, for I am not even acquainted with the man.'

"Then he rode over and began to rebuke the stranger with a six-shooter, and the stranger began to explain with another. When the pistols were emptied, the stranger resumed his work . . . and Mr. Harris rode by with a polite nod, homeward bound, with a bullet through one of his lungs, and several through his hips; and from them issued little rivulets of blood that coursed down the horse's sides and made the animal look quite picturesque." (*Roughing It*)

Twain's jocosity was typical of gold rush writing. Bret Harte also had a reputation as a humorist and used a similar hyperbole and deadpan irony to present violence. Harte was more of a Californian than Twain, having spent much of his youth in the state, and he had a more sympathetic and varied view of the landscape than Twain's. Harte's pine and cedar forests, usually well stocked with blue jays and squirrels, can have a sentimental sweetness approaching the Disney cartoon, but they can also contribute to his narratives in genuinely touching ways, as in this passage wherein a miner conveys the

STOREHOUSE RUIN AT JENNY LIND, 1983

THE BUTTE STORE NEAR MOKELUMNE HILL, 1983

coffin of his lynched partner to its grave: "The way led through Grizzly Canyon—by this time clothed in funereal drapery and shadows. The redwoods, burying their moccasoned [sic] feet in the red soil, stood in Indian-file along the track, trailing an uncouth benediction from their bending boughs upon the passing bier." (*Tennessee's Partner*)

By "redwood," I assume Harte means giant sequoia, which grows in the Mother Lode, instead of coast redwood, which doesn't.

As Harte is more appreciative of the California landscape than Twain, he also is more aware of the tremendous destruction that mining wreaked on it.

"There were huge fissures on the hillside, and displacements of the red soil, resembling more the chaos of some primary elemental upheaval than the work of man; while, half-way down, a long flume straddled its narrow body and disproportionate legs over the chasm, like an enormous fossil of some forgotten antediluvian. At every step smaller ditches crossed the road, hiding in their sallow depths unlovely streams that crept away to a clandestine union with the great yellow torrent below. Here and there the ruins of some cabin with the chimney alone left intact and the hearthstone open to the skies, gave such a flat contradiction to the poetic notion of 'lares' and 'penates' that the heart of the traveller must have collapsed as he gazed." (*M'liss*)

Though he admires them and regrets their destruction, Harte's foothills are still too tainted with violence and suffering for comfortable habitation. There is a sense of corruption, isolation, and foreboding, as in this description of the evening before a lynching: "It was a warm night. The cool breeze which usually sprang up with the going down of the sun behind the *chaparral*-crested mountain was that evening withheld from Sandy Bar. The little canyon was stifling with heated, resinous odors, and the decaying drift-wood on the Bar sent forth faint, sickening exhalations. The feverishness of day, and its fierce passions, still filled the camp. Lights moved restlessly along the bank of the river, striking no answering reflection from its tawny current. . . . And above all this, etched on the dark firmament, rose the Sierra, remote and passionless, crowned with remoter passionless stars." (*Tennessee's Partner*)

The best of Harte's stories, like *Tennessee's Partner*, about a man who tries to save his mining partner from lynching even though the partner is a thief, go beyond jauntiness and reach for compassionate transcendence of violent destiny. Harte doesn't quite reach it. His compassion remains more a salve to violence than a transcendence of it. Harte's characters are a little too distanced, a little too colorful, for readers to quite take them seriously. The deaths of Tennessee's partner and of the outcasts from Poker Flat provoke a tear, but they don't terrify. Harte cared about suffering: he was run out of northern California for newspaper editorials protesting the massacre of Indians. But he seems more concerned in his stories with resolving, even soothing, his own anger and horror than with arousing such feelings in his readers. He doesn't show us the massacres; he shows us Indian or half-breed infants who are helped by kindly miners or schoolmasters.

Another Mother Lode "humorist" did not share Twain's and Harte's propensity for burying bodies. Ambrose Bierce gleefully dug up the bodies. He had the honesty, or simply the spite, to write about mining life with only a sardonic pretense to jollity, and with no compassion. In stories such as *A Holy Terror* and *The Night-Doings at Deadman's*, Bierce laid on with lip-smacking relish the demoniac necrophilia that Twain flirted with: "The most attractive object in the world is the face we instinctively cover with a cloth. When it becomes still more attractive—fascinating—we put seven feet of earth above it." (*The Night-Doings at Deadman's*)

Both stories are about men who die from terror after intimate encounters with long-dead corpses—a disfigured prostitute's and a murdered Chinaman's. Both men are clearly responsible, through greed and cruelty, for their horrible ends: the one because he is digging up the prostitute's grave to stake a gold claim on it, the other because he not only murdered the Chinaman but desecrated his corpse. In both stories the jaunty, devil-may-care attitude Twain admired provokes savage, fateful retribution.

Bierce's foothills have a baleful vividness that suits his narratives. Having spent most of the Civil War as a scout for the Union Army, he had a highly developed sense of terrain, particularly of its military implications, its potentials for menace or advantage. The foothills' rugged ridges and gulches were perfectly suited for the eerie effects he sought: "It was a singularly sharp night, and clear as the heart of a diamond. Clear nights have a trick of being keen. In darkness you may be cold and not know it; when you see, you suffer. This night was bright enough to bite like a serpent. The moon was moving mysteriously along behind the giant pines crowning the South Mountain, striking a cold sparkle from the crusted snow, and bringing out against the black west the ghostly outlines of the Coast Range, beyond which lay the invisible Pacific. The snow had piled itself, in the open spaces along the bottom of the gulch,

SUTTER CREEK, 1983

OAKS AND CYPRESS NEAR SAN ANDREAS, 1983

into long ridges that seemed to heave, and into hills that appeared to toss and scatter spray. The spray was sunlight, twice reflected: dashed once from the moon, once from the snow." (*The Night-Doings at Deadman's*)

Bret Harte's description of a ghost town and its diggings seems almost sunny compared to Bierce's. Harte calls his town Smith's Pocket, a nice, colorful name. Bierce calls his Hurdy-Gurdy: ". . . a double row of forlorn shanties . . . seemed about to fall upon one another's neck to bewail their desolation; while about an equal number appeared to have straggled up the slope on either hand. . . . Most of these habitations were emaciated as by famine to the condition of mere skeletons, about which clung unlovely tatters of what might have been skin, but was really canvas. The little valley itself, torn and gashed by pick and shovel, was unhandsome with long, bending lines of decaying flume resting here and there upon the summits of sharp ridges, and stilting awkwardly across the intervals upon unhewn poles. . . . Wherever there remained a patch of the original soil a rank overgrowth of weeds and brambles had spread upon the scene, and from its dank, unwholesome shades the visitor curious in such matters might have obtained numberless souvenirs of the camp's former glory— fellowless boots mantled with green mould and plethoric of rotting leaves; an occasional old felt hat; desultory remnants of a flannel shirt; sardine boxes inhumanly mutilated and a surprising profusion of black bottles distributed with a truly catholic impartiality, everywhere." (*A Holy Terror*) Bierce does not follow his grim description with an introduction to the still-living inhabitants of the vicinity as Harte does. There are none.

"And now, when the town was fallen into the sere and yellow leaf of an unloved senility, the graveyard—though somewhat marred by time and circumstance . . . to say nothing of the devastating coyote—answered the humble needs of its denizens with reasonable completeness. It comprised a generous two acres of ground, which with commendable thrift but needless care had been selected for its mineral unworth, contained two or three skeleton trees (one of which had a stout lateral branch from which a weather-wasted rope still significantly dangled), half a hundred gravelly mounds, a score of rude headboards . . ." (*A Holy Terror*)

The current of destiny reaches a kind of culmination in the Mother Lode and in Ambrose Bierce. If Jeffers is its poet, Bierce is its avatar. His skull crushed by a bullet in the Civil War, he dominated western literary society for half a century with ferocious contempt, then disappeared into Mexico during the revolution with the apparent conscious intention of being put up against a wall and shot. "To be a Gringo in Mexico," he wrote his daughter, "that is euthanasia!" An experienced participant in violence (of which Twain and Harte were mostly spectators), Bierce is filled with a caustic anger that darkens his every perception. Humor is for him not a balm but a pretext for enticing readers to look at things they otherwise would evade. Landscape is not scenery improved by distance, as in Twain, or pathetic fallacy, as in Harte, but a menacing realm where little pockets of spectral cruelty, of psychic energy gone bad, wait to take vengeance on the violators, where hunters are killed by dreams or torn apart by invisible beasts.

Bierce is Jeffers's ranting, misanthropic side unrelieved by introspection. Indeed, Jeffers's last narrative poem, in which he looses his vengeful hatred, might have been written by Bierce. "The Double Axe" begins as a dead, rotting World War II GI returns from the Pacific to murder his father and rape his mother. It ends with a nuclear holocaust, an event that one suspects Bierce might have heralded with glee—the splitting of the atom as the final violation of nature, which sets in motion the final retribution.

It may seem paradoxical that two men so obsessed with violent American destiny should have spent most of their lives far from the centers of power. To some degree, Jeffers and Bierce seem to have shared the Arcadian delusion that destiny could be escaped, or at least diluted, by geographical isolation. Their strong feelings for natural landscape made them susceptible to such a delusion. It also forbade them, however, to turn their eyes away from the violent expansion that ravaged the landscape. Such ravages are all too conspicuous and long lasting in the dry California climate, like the lingering, murdered ghosts of the stories and poems.

ROCK OUTCROPPING EAST OF SAN ANDREAS, 1983

PROTECTED COTTONWOODS NEAR MARKLEEVILLE, 1983

VII
The
Great Mountains:
Beyond Arcadia

HORSE CABBAGE (MULLEIN), 1977

YOSEMITE BACKCOUNTRY, TUOLUMNE COUNTY
AUGUST 1972

We start out from Hetch Hetchy Reservoir, which is grim in the late summer heat—
a whitish bathtub ring of fallen water level on the glacier-carved cliffs, a jumble of
barren, silty rocks on the shore. It's a long, steep climb up the north wall of Tuolumne
Canyon, especially the first part, a series of switchbacks through sunstruck canyon
live oak woods. Canyon live oak just doesn't cast much of a shade, though it grows
quite tall. The tough little leaves seem to throw off light more than block it; they're
reflectors as much as absorbers. Standing under a canyon live oak is a little like standing
under a mirror or a sheet of aluminum—unrefreshing.

A mule team passes, going downhill, in a clatter of gear and a cloud of dust,
horseflies, and mule smell: a sight John Muir would have been familiar with. The
nineteenth century seems close on this carefully built foot and horse trail, after the
twentieth-century gigantism of dam and reservoir have receded.

The forest gets green and moist above the canyon rim, with tangles of ferns and
wildflowers in flats and hollows, big sugar and ponderosa pines and incense cedars.
We sit down a little off-trail for a rest and hear something galloping downhill,
pounding the trail like a horse. Suddenly a big black bear appears about five feet from
us, twitching its nose, evidently catching our scent. I say, "Hello, bear," and it turns
its head to us, eyelids drooping like an old dog's. It sniffs a moment, then abruptly
plunges downhill again, disappearing as quickly as it appeared. Later, we come upon
a cinnamon bear rubbing its back against a cedar.

We cross a ridge and drop into the meadow along Frog Creek, still so moist as to be
downright dank under their fringes of pine and fir, thick beds of corn lilies and cow
parsnips transpiring water with a profligacy that would break a San Joaquin Valley
farmer's heart. I hear what sounds like a spotted owl in the trees, high-pitched yapping.
It's getting late, but we continue along the ridgeline trail that leads to Jack Main
Canyon, stopping for the night in a little dry glade among firs and mountain hemlocks.

The next day we reach Tilden Lake and camp near the grassy, pathless east shore.
There are only a few groves of trees around the lake, and the alpine peaks of the Sierra
Crest are conspicuous to the northeast. The peaks don't lower or rear up savagely as do
the Rockies (at least, not from the relatively high elevation of their west side); they
look gentle and expansive, as though one could stroll to their tops easily. I drop my
pack at the lake and set out toward them almost involuntarily. Their warm colors
and soft textures have a tactile allure.

The going isn't as easy as it looks from a distance. There are boulders, bogs, willow thickets, brush fields, shifting piles of scree. The ground doesn't have a surface here as it does lower down, where conifer needles accumulate to form a level duff. Here there are only little patches of soil among the rocks, and every one of these patches seems densely grown with tough, lush plants, so that the only surfaces one can really step on are the not very stable rocks. I know how a giant would feel trying to pick his way through a boulder-strewn forest that came up to his calves, his thighs, sometimes his waist. There's a bewildering diversity of plants, not only the little wildflowers one would expect on subalpine terrain, but big leafy herbs and grasses and bushes—dwarf maple, elderberry, bitter cherry, spiraea, creamberry, mountain ash—many of them getting their first tinges of fall reds and yellows, which in combination with the wildflowers makes the landscape riotously colorful.

It's silent except for the splash of water and the occasional rattle of a stone, but there's animal life too: bees and butterflies and the little rosy finches that spend almost their entire lives among the peaks. They seem less shy than birds lower down, and I get some fairly close looks at them as they perch momentarily on rocks, in between arcing flights above the horizon. I watch out for wolverine, pika, varying hare, or other boreal creatures.

There's a chill in this landscape that belies its warm colors, and it deepens through the afternoon as though a river of winter air is flowing down the canyon bottom, a river that rises as the sun sinks. I turn around when the peaks start to get rosy, and it gets very cold indeed when the sunlight fails. The grass around the lake is already soggy with dew when I get back.

PINE SEEDLING AND PENSTEMON IN GRANITE, SONORA PASS, 1983

SOUTH PEAKS, WHITNEY PORTAL, 1973

THE PHYSICAL SCARS of the gold rush are healing. The Mother Lode has become rather quaint and sleepy, as though to fulfill Twain's and Harte's yearning to salve the raw meanness of history. Hardly anyone reads Ambrose Bierce today, and there aren't town festivals commemorating *his* stories. The foothills are no longer a destination, except for moderate numbers of retirees, commuters, hippies, and others seeking the country life. Instead, the foothills have become a way station on a pilgrimage taken every year by as many people as participated in the gold rush, and for precisely the opposite purpose. Where the miners went to the hills to suffer and get rich, the present-day pilgrims go to the mountains above the hills to enjoy themselves, and to spend enough money doing so to make an oldtime prospector's eyes protrude.

Even if the sums the pilgrims spend didn't give the old miner a shock, the things they spend them to *do* certainly would. Walking across mountains with heavy packs, running dangerous rivers in flimsy boats, spending days or weeks without fresh food, shivering and cowering in thunderstorms—these were all hardships miners had to endure. But to seek them for amusement! Something happened to Western civilization in the late nineteenth century, and the California mountains had a lot to do with it.

Mountains had never been very popular with Western civilization before the nineteenth century. They were too hard to control. True, they had resources—timber, water, game, pasturage—but they tended to be too rugged and inaccessible for permanent, safe habitation; so heavily populated and civilized states like ancient Rome had to put up with mountains in their very backyards that were full of wild beasts, brigands, and other unregulated items. If rich merchants and officials wanted to get from one side of Italy to the other, they had to use roads whereon one of their pack animals might conceivably be eaten by a bear, an event not conducive to decorum.

The old agrarian societies had a view of nature that was rather the opposite of the modern, evolutionary one. Where evolution sees wild nature as the primal state from which domestication has grown, ancient societies tended to see wild nature as a corruption of a primal, domesticated state of nature. Adam and Eve lived in a garden where the lion lay down with the lamb. Predation and the other functions of wild nature did not come about until the fall and expulsion. The farm was the primal state, not the forest. This ancient view still lives in the modern, Arcadian tendency, which seeks in a return to agrarian simplicity a kind of primal harmony, an end to the disturbing competition and mutability of an evolutionary world.

Ancient Rome did not yearn for a technological utopia, as many Americans do, but longed for a prehistorical Golden Age, in which the comfortable stability of the old-fashioned country estate would be permanently reestablished. The Romans did what they could to bring back the Golden Age by founding the empire and building the most extensive system of roads ever. But the mountains remained wild, unredeemed. They remained wild after Rome fell, and throughout various succeeding societies that based their aspirations on the Roman model. Even stripped of trees and eaten down to bare rock by sheep and goats, the mountains remained wolf haunted, living reproaches to a hopeful view of nature as divinely, benignly created for human comfort and convenience.

A horror of mountains persisted popularly until the late eighteenth century, when traveling ladies would pull down the blinds of their carriages to be spared a distressing view of the Alps. Then, suddenly, the mountains became fashionable. Picture galleries were full of crags and peaks, and the undisciplined sound of mountain torrents echoed in symphonies and sonatas. The sudden reversal of fashion was the outcome of several centuries of developing science, industry, and nation states, which gave civilization an increased control over mountains at the same time they provided a radical new way of seeing them.

Natural philosophers and poets found they could stroll about the Alps at leisure instead of hurrying anxiously across them as their Renaissance and Enlightenment counterparts largely had. New scientific theories inclined them to look at the mountains not only as a backdrop for human aspirations but as phenomena interesting in themselves. Mountains were not simply jumbles of rock thrown up during the Flood, but products of comprehensible geological forces; they had a life of their own, were rising, eroding, developing. Growing industrial wealth gave spectators a new appreciation for the sheer mechanical grandeur of mountains, their superlatives of height, mass, slope. Nature's capacity to do mechanical work was gaining new respect as more and more mill wheels turned.

Yet the new fashion was not wholly, or even chiefly, utilitarian. (Our ancestors did not hold the useful and the beautiful as rigidly apart as we do.) It

TUOLUMNE RIVER ABOVE SONORA, 1983

NORTH LAKE, EASTERN SIERRA, 1983

viewed mountain superlatives as things to be aspired to as well as used. Where the Arcadian valued nature chiefly as a comfortable, attractive setting for society, the new current of thought (which was first called the Sublime, then, less appropriately, the Romantic) began to see intrinsic beauty in wild nature —tranquillity, grandeur, mystery, purity—qualities which might improve the human world. Dawning evolutionary theories abetted this view by implying a much more ancient existence for precivilized, indeed prehuman, nature than was previously imagined.

Yet the Sublime had its limitations in Europe, where even the remotest massifs showed considerable civilized influence. Such pioneer enthusiasts of the Sublime as William Wordsworth could not ignore the "still, sad music of humanity" even while traipsing about the remote Lake Country, exulting in rills and crags. The music was indeed sad; rural Britain was thronged with landless agricultural laborers who lived mainly on cabbage and oatmeal, whose only hopes for betterment lay in moving to the manufacturing centers that Wordsworth and his friends justifiably found ghastly, or in emigration. One might say that the rural poor and the Sublime had the same problem—overpopulation. So the Sublime joined a certain segment of the rural poor and emigrated.

This is more than a metaphor. Like the spirit of a departed lama, the Sublime seems to have entered into the flesh of a child born in Scotland in 1837, who then emigrated with his rural family to America. I've seen no more convincing explanation than this admittedly Tantric and fantastic one of how John Muir evolved from the son of bigoted, Calvinist Scottish farmers into the most effective exponent of the Sublime the world has yet produced.

Muir's love of wilderness was nourished early by the Scottish mountains, but it's doubtful that even he could have developed the concept of the Sublime as fully as he did if he hadn't found the California mountains. There is probably nowhere else in the world where the "otherness" of nature exists in such an attractive, healthful, safe, and relatively undamaged form as in the great California mountains, the Sierra Nevada in particular, but also the Klamaths to the northwest, the Cascades to the north, and various ranges to the south. They are not too hot, not too cold; not too wet, not too dry; not too fecund, not too sterile. Camping in them brings to mind (to my mind at least) odd parallels with fine hotels. The accommodations are in the very best of taste, the architecture airy but solid, the grounds green and flowery. The water is pure, the smells pleasant and appetizing. There are no large quantities of biting insects, almost no lurking diseases. There is sparkling granite to sit on, clear lakes to swim in, soft beds of fir needles to sleep on. When Muir refers to God in his writing, which is pretty often, the divine authority sounds like a highly thoughtful and tasteful builder and landlord who for some reason is absentee, confidently leaving it to his clients to keep the place up.

It may seem paradoxical that a place so pleasant as the Sierra should have fostered a view of nature as *not* created solely for human comfort and convenience. But the landlord has made it clear, through intensely subarctic winter storms and an absence of agricultural soils, that the property is a resort, not a residence. John Muir did not chafe at the landlord's restrictions, even the most hair-raising ones. Avalanches were to be ridden like surf; earthquakes and hurricanes to be enjoyed from the tops of the tallest available trees; autumn nights to be passed sleeping in the bushes without a blanket. John Muir did not only admire the qualities of wild nature; he tried very strenuously, and with some success, to emulate them.

Muir contradicts Twain's contention that the California mountains have charm only at a distance as though they were in direct debate: "Generally, when looking for the first time . . . the inexperienced observer is oppressed by the incomprehensible grandeur, variety, and abundance of the mountains rising shoulder to shoulder beyond the reach of vision; and it is only after they have been studied one by one, long and lovingly, that their far-reaching harmonies become manifest. Then, penetrate the wilderness where you may, the main telling features, to which all the surrounding topography is subordinate, are quickly perceived, and the most complicated clusters of peaks stand revealed harmoniously correlated and fashioned like works of art. . . . The cañons, too, some of them a mile deep, mazing wildly through the mighty host of mountains, however lawless and ungovernable at first sight they appear, are at length recognized as the necessary effects of causes which followed each other in harmonious sequence—Nature's poems carved on tables of stone—the simplest and most emphatic of her glacial compositions." (*The Mountains of California*)

Where Twain finds monotony in the California forests, Muir finds superlative diversity: "Coniferous trees, in general, seldom possess individual character, such as is manifest among Oaks and Elms. But the California forests are made up of a greater number of distinct species than any other in the world.

COTTONWOODS IN EARLY FALL, SONORA PASS, 1983

TARN, TIOGA PASS, 1977

And in them we find, not only a marked differentiation into special groups, but also a marked individuality in almost every tree, giving rise to storm effects indescribably glorious."

Of course, Muir's descriptions are just as subjective as Twain's. Still, they are based on much more experience than Twain's. I believe it is quite possible that no other human being has experienced natural landscape as intensely and fully as Muir did. The American wilderness was explored by many fearless men and by fair numbers of sensitive ones, but Muir seems to have been both fearless and sensitive, which permitted him an unprecedented intimacy with landscape. Readers are sometimes led by his effusively Victorian prose, his avowals of bosom friendship with trees and birds, into thinking him a sentimentalist. But no sentimentalist could have undergone the hardships and dangers Muir not only underwent but welcomed in seeking the other that lives in nature.

Muir's emotional appetite for wild landscape was equaled by his hunger to comprehend its mechanics—the force of water or ice on rock, of tree roots on soil. He combined science and art in a way that is peculiar to the Sublime viewpoint. His books are at once ecstatic rhapsodies and accounts of scientific researches. He does not approach landscape as a backdrop upon which human concerns are reflected but as a source of revelation. Muir's books are sermons as well as explorations; he exhorts readers to shake off the habituated numbness of civilized life and seek an intense relationship with nature.

"We are now in the mountains and they are in us, kindling enthusiasm, making every nerve quiver, filling every pore and cell of us. Our flesh and bone tabernacle seems transparent as glass to the beauty about us, as if truly a part of it, thrilling with the air and trees, streams and rocks, in the waves of the sun —a part of all nature, neither old nor young, sick nor well, but immortal. . . . How glorious a conversion, so complete and wholesome is it, scarce memory enough of old bondage days left as a standpoint to view it from! In this newness of life we seem to have been so always." (*My First Summer in the Sierra*)

Muir's writing has an exceptional power to convey the sense of wholesomeness and invigoration he got from the mountains. I started reading him on my lunch breaks when I was driving a taxi in San Francisco, and his descriptions of trees and rocks made me hungry; they made a cheese sandwich and some carrot sticks seem like a banquet. I felt as though I were eating the mountains in some mildly sacramental way, and I knew I wouldn't be satisfied until I got up there to devour them in the flesh.

123

"Of all the world's eighty or ninety species of pine trees, the Sugar Pine (*Pinus Lambertiana*) is king. . . . The largest specimens are commonly about 220 feet high and from six to eight feet in diameter four feet from the ground, though some grand old patriarch may be met here and there that has enjoyed six or eight centuries of storms and attained a thickness of ten or even twelve feet, still sweet and fresh in every fiber. . . . How well they sing in the wind, and how strikingly harmonious an effect is made by the long cylindrical cones, depending loosely from the ends of the long branches! The cones are about fifteen to eighteen inches long, and three in diameter; green, shaded with dark purple on their sunward sides. They are ripe in September and October of the second year from the flower. Then the flat, thin scales open and the seeds take wing, but the empty cones become still more beautiful and effective as decorations, for their diameter is nearly doubled by the spreading of the scales, and their color changes to yellowish brown while they remain, swinging on the tree all the following winter and summer, and continue effectively beautiful even on the ground many years after they fall. The wood is deliciously fragrant, fine in grain and texture and creamy yellow, as if formed of condensed sunbeams." (*The Yosemite*)

Muir's faith in the improving propensities of wild nature might be dismissed as an example of old-fashioned nineteenth-century progressivism. There certainly is an element of the progressive booster in the Muir that hobnobbed with Teddy Roosevelt and Thomas Edison. Robinson Jeffers was much less sanguine than Muir about the human capacity for improvement through science and nature. Jeffers's pessimism was undoubtedly deepened by the wars and massacres of the twentieth century; still, it doesn't really seem more modern than Muir's optimism. Jeffers's view of humanity was curiously static and archaic: a cyclic mythos of tribes that grow into republics that explode into empires that decline into barbarous tribalism, from which the cycle resumes. In this, Jeffers's outlook is more Arcadian than Sublime. Believing in evolution in nature, he still doubts the capacity of humanity to evolve new ways of living. The time of the Greek republics is the Golden Age from which history must decline.

A more recent exponent of the Sublime in the California mountains has drawn a cautious optimism resembling Muir's from the study of anthropology, a science less well developed in Muir's day. Anthropology has placed human culture in an evolutionary perspective for the twentieth century as geology

GLACIAL PAVEMENT, CARSON PASS, 1983

ROUND VALLEY AND MOUNT TOM, 1973

placed the biosphere so in the nineteenth. It has allowed poet Gary Snyder to look back past Arcadian golden ages to prehistoric cultures profoundly unlike civilization and to see hope in the human plasticity science has discovered. By looking at human history not only in the farmers, herders, and urbanites of the written record but in the less populous hunters, gatherers, and gardeners who long preceded them (people whom Jeffers characteristically calls "the weak hunters"), Snyder proposes an alternative to cyclic pessimism. He sees the violent destinies of civilization not as the main current of humanity but as a brief, recent detour from an evolution that has largely been in harmony with nature, a detour that may well lead over a cliff, but that still does not condemn (or exalt) humanity as separate.

"The evidence of anthropology is that countless men and women, through history and pre-history, have experienced a deep sense of communion and communication with nature and with specific non-human beings." (*The Old Ways*)

Snyder, who lived and worked in the Sierra like Muir, writes about it in a similar intimate, appetizing way:

> foxtail pine with a
> clipped curve-back cluster of tight
>   five needle bunches
>   the rough red bark scale
> and jigsaw pieces sloughed off
>   scattered on the ground.
> —what am I doing saying "foxtail pine"?
> these conifers whose home was ice
> age tundra, taiga, they of the
>   naked sperm
> do whitebark pine and white pine seem the same?
>
>   a sort of tree
>   its leaves are needles
>   like a fox's brush
> (I call him fox because he looks that way)
>   and call this other thing, a
>   foxtail pine.
>
>   ("Foxtail Pine")

Wilderness is not a distant, empty place for Muir and Snyder. They both have the workmanlike, friendly attitude toward it that some Americans learned from the Indians, the confidence that everything one wants in the way of business or pleasure can be gotten in the wilderness without any particular need to combat or overcome it, simply by observing it and understanding it. Wilderness is an ally and teacher for Muir and Snyder, an attitude they probably learned to a great extent from growing up on backwoods farms in Wisconsin and Washington, respectively.

For Jeffers, who grew up in more genteel surroundings, wilderness is more distant, noble and beautiful, but still a backdrop to cyclic agonies. It shrinks into bare rock gullies as spreading empires devour the earth, then expands again as empires collapse in violent destiny. This is, of course, a basic outline of history. Civilizations have traditionally devoured their wilderness—timber, wildlife, fertile soil, clean water—then exploded into conquering hordes or subsided into fitful sleeps of poverty. But the Sublime viewpoint does not see the cycle as inevitable. It sees at least the possibility that a wilderness stabilized and safeguarded through political action could act in its turn as a stabilizing and safeguarding influence on human cultures, as it has acted through most of humanity's time on earth.

MORNING SKY, SONORA PASS, 1977

ALKALI LAKE, OWENS VALLEY, 1973

VIII
The Desert:
Bloom and Bust

SAN JACINTO MOUNTAINS, 1976

They would call this canyon "badlands" if the land around it weren't the Mojave Desert, itself a consummate "badland." The canyon is a forbidding place even in a desert, a labyrinth of grotesquely eroded mudstones left over from some ancient lakebed. It emerges from the desert's more normal flat valley floors and naked rock ranges like a mirage, a manifestation of some deeply hallucinatory potential of physical reality. It is as though the earth were making a joke, and not a very innocent or lighthearted joke.

One might hope that the stiff, relentless wind blowing from the fogbound coast across Walker Pass would be moderated by the canyon's red rock cliffs; but it is merely deflected, sent rushing up and down the narrow side canyons, buffeting across the flats, spinning around the stacks and pipes and domes and caps of mudstone. It can't be escaped, even in the caves formed where great organ pipe shapes of red rock have collapsed inward, making doors and windows so palatial-looking that one half-expects to find inlaid floors and tiled fountains inside them instead of piles of mud and rubble and dry weeds shaken by the wind.

The soil under the cliffs is bare of plants, a ceramic pavement of brick red or gray green clay, but sandy stretches on the canyon floor between them bear creosote bushes, Joshua trees, cholla cactuses, ephedras, and an array of spring wildflowers that seems reassuringly normal amid the geological surrealism. A patch of yellow on a seep below one cliff is a colony of monkey flowers, familiar from seeps all over California. Miniature golden composites and pink and white phloxes and purple monkey flowers hug the sand; above them rise spikes and bursts of blossom: big, pale violet evening prim-roses, smaller white-and-brick-red evening primroses, deep violet gilias, pale violet asters, purple phacelias, baby blue larkspurs, royal blue lupines, scarlet paintbrushes, magenta beavertail cactus flowers, and, unexpectedly, giant docks with lush green leaves and deep red seed heads, a species aptly called "desert rhubarb."

The flowers would be even showier if large swaths of the canyon floor weren't denuded by off-road vehicle tracks, which crisscross and meander and converge with a frenetic randomness that does not, actually, seem so out of place in this frenetic, random erosional landscape. The abrasion of wind and water on mudstone seems not unrelated to the more abrupt grinding of rubber. Both are mechanical phenomena to which the more complicated operations of life, of shrubs and flowers and desert lizards, must try to adapt.

133

The wheel tracks don't even stop when I venture up a side canyon so narrow and boulder strewn and potholed that it is hard enough going on foot. Two great blocks of mudstone stand on either side of the canyon's opening, like ferocious idols at a temple gate. One is yellowish gray, beetling like the skull of a hydrocephalic giant; the other is brick red, lean and prognathous as a crocodile's jaw. Both shapes eventually seem tame compared to some of the howling petrological extravaganzas farther up the canyon. I follow it for a long time, until the last sunlight leaves. It's hard to stop; the suggestive peculiarity of the mudstone shapes is enchanting. They seem to act directly on my mind, to knead and stretch it, squeezing aside the comfortable but cumbersome furniture of normal perception.

It's an unsettling feeling at first, then exhilarating, and oddly calming, perhaps out of relief that my mind can adapt to the strangeness. After all, the brush rabbits and pack rats live happily enough among these rocks that seem always to be trying to shift and deliquesce into other shapes, which suggests that life is somehow a match for the vagaries of rock, for the latent unpredictability and violence of nonlife. The brown-and-white-feathered shape of a prairie falcon that flies away from a ledge of red snaggle teeth and vaguely erotic Indian temple shapes as I turn a corner seems beautifully substantial and harmonious.

The canyon floor finally becomes so choked with boulders that even the tire tracks give up, and I climb a ridge to get the last rays of sunlight. A pair of Say's phoebes is mating among phallic spires of green mudstone, and mourning doves and sparrows are singing, undaunted by the windy desolation. The moon rises to the east in a sky of extraordinary blueness. I retrace my steps to the main canyon, where the red cliffs loom several hundred feet overhead. A pair of golden eagles evidently is nesting in them. I watch them carrying sticks and branches to recesses far up the cliff. The wind gets very cold without the sun, but the moonlight is so bright that the flowers still seem warmly incandescent against the darkening sand.

CALIFORNIA is about a quarter desert, from the sagebrush and shadscale steppe of the Great Basin in the northeast to the cactus and creosote bush of the Mojave and Sonoran deserts in the southeast. The desert is largely a product of the great mountains, which grab most of the precipitation from Pacific storms, and this seems appropriate. Desert raises in ultimate terms the question raised by Muir and Snyder in the mountains, whether humanity can break out of the boom-and-bust cycles of civilized history and evolve more stable, creative relationships with the earth. Desert civilizations have been especially susceptible to boom-and-bust cycles because they've been based on irrigation systems easily disrupted by invaders or by various environmental problems such as siltation or salinization.

Despite its instability, desert civilization is the prototype of urban civilization as we know it. Sumeria, the first large city-state, was founded on irrigation and fell because of the gradual destruction of its irrigation system. Urban civilization's fundamental belief that it survives by artifice, by cleverly working its will on a malign but stupid nature, has its origin and highest expression in the desert empire. The act of bringing water to an apparently barren soil and creating a complex culture on it gives the irrigator an unprecedented sense of power and autonomy. Neither water nor soil is created by the irrigator, of course, but the wealth that arises from their synthesis makes them *seem* a human creation, a human possession.

The desert empire that has arisen in California and other parts of the American Southwest is probably the most artificial ever, the cleverest, the most engineered. At the same time the landscape around this enclave of canals, pipelines, freeways, reservoirs, and exploding suburbs is the most savage in North America outside the far north. Only muskeg and tundra offer greater challenges to human survival than the desert. Fiction writers have approached desert and tundra similarly, as places where civilized violence and acquisitiveness meet

135

their match. Jack London's Klondike prospectors are very like Frank Norris's murderous dentist in *McTeague*: both find that their own ruthlessness is no help against a night above the Arctic Circle or an afternoon in Death Valley.

"The sun rose higher; hour by hour as the dentist tramped steadily on, the heat increased. The baked, dry sand crackled into innumerable tiny flakes under his feet. The twigs of the sagebrush snapped like brittle pipestems as he pushed through them. It grew hotter. At eleven the earth was like the surface of a furnace; the air, as McTeague breathed it in, was hot to his lips and the roof of his mouth. The sun was a disk of molten brass swimming in the burnt-out blue of the sky. McTeague stripped off his woolen shirt, and even unbuttoned his flannel undershirt, tying a handkerchief loosely around his neck.

"The heat grew steadily fiercer; all distant objects were visibly shimmering and palpitating under it. At noon a mirage appeared on the hills to the northwest. McTeague halted the mule and drank from the tepid water in the canteen. . . . As soon as he ceased his tramp and the noise of his crunching, grinding footsteps died away, the silence, vast, illimitable, enfolded him like an immeasurable tide. From all that gigantic landscape, that colossal reach of baking sand, there arose not a single sound. Not a twig rattled, not an insect hummed, not a bird or beast invaded that huge solitude with call or cry. Everything as far as the eye could reach . . . lay inert, absolutely quiet and moveless under the remorseless scourge of the noon sun. The very shadows shrank away, hiding under sagebushes, retreating to the farthest nooks and crevices in the canyons of the hills. All the world was one gigantic blinding glare, silent, motionless." (*McTeague*)

The traditional civilized response to the desert's extreme otherness has been to push it aside as completely as possible, "to make the desert bloom." The artificial garden civilization in the desert is an ultimate expression of the Arcadian ideal, a reconstruction of Eden from the very desert into which humanity's fallen parents were cast out. The idea of such a reconstruction was a very conscious element of America's settlement of desert regions, particularly for religious sects such as the Mormons, but also for secular society. It underlies the Bureau of Reclamation's bizarrely illogical name, since "reclamation" means restoration to use, and there is no evidence that the Colorado River was used to support cities of millions of people before the bureau rose up to smite it with dams and diversion. The bureau uses "reclamation" in a spiritual sense, not a physical one (odd that an agency so pragmatic in function should

136

RIDGELINES, ZABRISKIE POINT, DEATH VALLEY, 1983

ALABAMA HILLS AND EASTERN SIERRA, 1973

be so metaphysical in conception)—that a world originally created solely for human use should be reclaimed from wilderness and restored to that sole use.

Steinbeck's Arcadia-seeking Joads see the desert as it has been seen by the majority of westward migrating Americans: "The truck took the road and moved up the long hill, through the broken, rotten rock. The engine boiled very soon and Tom slowed down and took it easy. Up the long slope, winding and twisting through dead country, burned white and grey, and no hint of life in it. Once Tom stopped for a few moments to let the engine cool, and then he travelled on. They topped the pass while the sun was still up, and looked down on the desert—black cinder mountains in the distance, and the yellow sun reflected on the grey desert. The little starved bushes, sage and greasewood, threw bold shadows on the sand and bits of rock." (*The Grapes of Wrath*)

Yet the desert unreclaimed is not as hostile to life as Norris's and Steinbeck's descriptions make it seem. Indeed, Norris's antihero McTeague promptly encounters life even in that "gigantic, blinding glare" of Death Valley.

" 'Ain't it *ever* going to let up?' groaned the dentist, rolling his eyes at the sky of hot-blue brass. Then, as he spoke, the stillness was abruptly stabbed through and through by a shrill sound that seemed to come from all sides at once. It ceased; then, as McTeague took another forward step, began again with the suddenness of a blow, shriller, nearer at hand, a hideous, prolonged note that brought both man and mule to an instant halt.

" 'I know what *that* is,' exclaimed the dentist. His eyes searched the ground swiftly until he saw what he expected he should see—the round thick coil, the slowly waving clover-shaped head and erect whirring tail with its vibrant rattles."

From the Arcadian viewpoint, the rattlesnake, the desert viper, is the epitome of unredeemed nature's malignity and stupidity, a creature whose only function is to venomously bite the unwary walker. From the evolutionary viewpoint, however, the rattlesnake is simply indifferent, not malign, and extremely ingenious, an array of adaptive functions that are far from stupid. The rattles are evolved not to frighten people but to warn blundering, large animals; the venom not to injure people but to quickly immobilize nimble rodent prey. From the evolutionary viewpoint, the indifferent heat and aridity of the desert are redeemed by the extraordinary ingenuity of its life, which has made a comfortable home from a place that seems hostile and deadly to a nonadapted civilization.

139

I remember how surprised I was, on first venturing into the sagebrush hills and shadscale flats east of the mountains, to find just as much animal life, perhaps more, than in the lush green forests and meadows of the Sierra. In daytime the scrub was full of birds—mountain bluebirds, sparrows, magpies, jays, hawks, Say's phoebes, pipits. The sand was laced with bobcat, deer, coyote, jackrabbit, rodent, lizard, and snake tracks. At twilight the scrub was even more densely occupied by the bobbing, pale shapes of kangaroo rats, and the hills resounded with poorwill and coyote cries, making for a livelier night than the frosty mountain one.

No writer has captured the almost perverse ingenuity and fecundity of California desert life better than Mary Austin. From the amount of wild animal activity she describes in *The Land of Little Rain,* she might have been living in a different country from the one through which air-conditioned sedans now obliviously speed. But the paucity of desert vegetation can be revealing instead of depressing if one is interested, and Mary Austin certainly was. Not even John Muir had as good an eye for the secret, subtle lives of wild beings as she.

"Go as far as you dare in the heart of a lonely land, you cannot go so far that life and death are not before you. Painted lizards slip in and out of rock crevices, and pant on the white hot sands. Birds, hummingbirds even, nest in the cactus scrub; woodpeckers befriend the demoniac yuccas; out of the stark, treeless waste rings the music of the night-singing mockingbird."

Even the paucity of vegetation is an ingenious adaptation to desert conditions. "There is neither poverty of soil nor species to account for the sparseness of desert growth, but simply that each plant requires more room. So much earth must be preempted to extract so much moisture. The real struggle for existence, the real brain of the plant, is underground; above there is room for a rounded perfect growth. In Death Valley, reputed the very core of desolation, are nearly two hundred identified species."

"The desert floras shame us with their cheerful adaptations to the seasonal limitations. Their whole duty is to flower and fruit, and they do it hardly, or with tropical luxuriance, as the rain admits. It is recorded in the report of the Death Valley expedition that after a year of abundant rains, on the Colorado desert was found a specimen of Amaranthus ten feet high. A year later the same species in the same place matured in the drought at four inches."

For Austin the desert is not an emptiness but a place of enormous possibility, which invites the human visitor to survive and prosper by observation and

OWENS RIVER, BENTON CROSSING, 1973

SENTINEL PEAK FROM ABOVE FURNACE CREEK, DEATH VALLEY, 1983

wisdom. It is an invitation that nature incessantly makes to all evolving beings. It is not, moreover, an invitation that can be ignored with impunity.

"There are many areas in the desert where drinkable water lies within a few feet of the surface, indicated by the mesquite and the bunch grass (*Sporobolus airoides*). It is this nearness of unimagined help that makes the tragedy of desert deaths. It is related that the final breakdown of that hapless party that gave Death Valley its forbidding name occurred in a locality where shallow wells would have saved them. . . . To underestimate one's thirst, to pass a given landmark to the right or left, to find a dry spring where one looked for running water—there is no help for any of these things."

"Making the desert bloom" is as great a misnomer as the Bureau of "Reclamation." The desert blooms without civilized help when ample rains bring out its considerable diversity and abundance of native wildflowers. It is not the desert that blooms in the cotton and melon fields of the Imperial Valley or the gardens of Palm Springs. The desert no longer exists in such places; it has been replaced.

As history shows, the replacement is an unstable one. If civilization, having obliterated the living, evolving desert, itself disappears, then the bare rock and sand remaining will be all the more forbidding to humanity. We can't know what ecological arrangements may have existed on the Mesopotamian plain before Sumeria reduced it to salt flats and rubble. We do know that various Indian tribes inhabited the California desert for thousands of years before Western civilization arrived to "reclaim" it. They planted some irrigated crops but derived most of their sustenance from wild plants and animals.

The desert is the only natural California landscape that cannot be regarded with some favor from an Arcadian viewpoint. Even the shaggy mountains can serve a Golden Age as sheep pasture and timber supply and watershed. But the desert must be erased and "reclaimed" if classical agrarian civilization is to control the entire earth. On the other hand, no other landscape is better suited to the viewpoint of the Sublime than desert. Even more than mountains, it bares the titanic ecological and geological forces that impel evolution. Even more than mountains, it encompasses superlatives of silence, solitude, and mystery. Frank Norris's description of morning in Death Valley is an exemplar of sublimity: "The day was magnificent. From horizon to horizon was one vast span of blue, whitening as it dipped earthward. Miles upon miles to the east and southeast the desert unrolled itself, white, naked, inhospitable, palpitating and

143

shimmering under the sun, unbroken by so much as a rock or cactus stump. In the distance it assumed all manner of faint colors, pink, purple, and pale orange. To the west rose the Panamint Range, sparsely sprinkled with gray sagebrush; here the earths and sands were yellow, ochre, and rich, deep red, the hollows and canyons picked out with intense blue shadows. It seemed strange that such barrenness could exhibit this radiance of color, but nothing could have been more beautiful than the deep red of the higher bluffs and ridges, seamed with purple shadows, standing sharply out against the pale blue-whiteness of the horizon." (*McTeague*)

As Mary Austin says, the desert shames us with a beauty and ingenuity that is not ours. This is the essence of the Sublime viewpoint: not to look down upon wild nature as a welter of inert, unredeemed resources, but to look up to it as a realm of unexpected possibilities, of Muir's "far-reaching harmonies." The less obvious use a landscape has to human culture, the greater the possibility of evolutionary change. From this viewpoint, to treat the desert as an emptiness to push aside, or, failing that, to race motorcycles on, is to insult the human potential as well as the desert's strange beauty.

SANDSTONE, WALKER PASS, 1972

IT IS SIGNIFICANT that the stages by which Californians explore a transect of their landscape move in the opposite direction from America's classic westward progress. Most Californians live near the coast; there is no farther westward for them to go, literally or figuratively. To explore, they must move east, either toward the compass east of the Atlantic and Europe, or toward the cultural east of the Orient. This makes for a different exploration than the traditional American one, which begins in poverty and constriction—of old Europe or the Atlantic colonies—and pushes toward wealth and liberty. To explore their landscape, Californians leave the ease and abundance of "the Coast" and push inward, toward the physical limits of the mountains, the parsimony of the deserts. Or, as Snyder and others have done, they leave the accumulated wealth of Western civilization and push "back" toward the frugalities of Oriental meditation philosophies and prehistoric tribal consciousness.

This west to east tendency has been perceived as subversive by guardians of traditional Occidental values, who see civilized destiny as one of continual expansion, forward movement. Indeed, it does run counter to the history of European peoples over at least the past five thousand years, a history characterized by movement toward the setting sun. It's a strange history when one thinks about it: white-skinned tribes emerging from a long glacial winter in the shadow of the Caucasus, then wandering toward sunset through all those centuries, as though hypnotized, as though an impression of the sinking fireball (fear of losing it to glacial darkness?) is burned into their minds' eyes. The impression is so deep, it seems, that when finally confronted by geographical limits, Americans have made a virtual state religion of space travel, of following the celestial light right off the planet, raising rockets skyward in somewhat the same spirit that the ancient Egyptians raised pyramids, as a way of voyaging to worlds beyond earthly mortality, the astronaut in his capsule and the pharaoh in his spirit boat both setting out to find the sun god in his star palace.

The trouble with state religions is that they are not very democratic. Pyramids and rockets are not for ordinary people, except vicariously. Ordinary

Egyptians were buried with little toy spirit boats; Americans can watch lift-off on television. But America also has a populist pioneer tradition; Americans still are taught to be restless and wander at the same time they are taught to settle down and pay taxes. I remember how contemptuous my grandmother was (a suffragette in her youth) of the idea of spending one's whole life in the town one grew up in. When your *grandmother* tells you to be restless, it really means something.

Ordinary Americans can't go to the stars yet feel called upon to go places. Many have gone to California. After that, what? The California dilemma of standing at the geographical limit of a venerable historical expansion is that of America as a whole, of the West as a whole. California is the last in the long series of successful Western conquests; it's no wonder its literature tends to hark back to that of ancient Greece, one of those earlier conquests by the sun-worshiping tribes. Eastern critics who see in California writing merely a sentimental glorification of primitivism don't know their classics well enough. The violent destiny that obsessed Jeffers and London was not their invention. They *saw* the violence in a particularly sharp and vivid way because the weight of nineteenth-century American technology condensed a conquest that earlier would have taken centuries (as did the colonization of America's Atlantic Coast) into a few dozen years.

California also is a reminder, with its mountains and deserts, that the biosphere is still a fundamentally wild environment. The dilemma of California is not just that of the West but of humanity, which cannot conquer the biosphere although it has been conquering its neighbors, human and otherwise, ever since it invented weapons, and probably before, given the tendency of newly evolved organisms to expand into new habitats. It is the dilemma of the pioneer organism, which modifies the new habitats it "conquers" until they become inhospitable for it, so that it must continually expand its conquests. If such an organism is so successful as to expand into all available habitats, it has two evolutionary options. It can become an extinct pioneer organism or evolve a new, nonpioneer form. Sometimes it seems that human history will have to parallel that of the first (hypothetical) predatory bacteria, which soon after evolving ate up almost all the nonpredatory bacteria, then nearly became extinct themselves.

I hope the world will never be that simple again. Humans have at least the possibility of more complex responses to evolutionary dilemmas than bacteria.

Shooting off spaceships is one. There may be others, less fantastic and elitist. People are going to have to keep living on the earth, and there's still quite a lot of it worth exploring. No matter how many previous generations have inhabited it, no matter how many definitive studies have been done, it's still a new place to the living.

Literature, much of which is the words of dead people, may seem a poor medium for seeing the world anew. But *good* literature is largely a record of very new and fresh visions of the world and can be a powerful incentive to seeing as well as a substitute for it. I would not have seen California as I have without the incentive of its literature. The fact that I was not a pioneer, was crossing old ground, going backward in a sense, did not make it less new for me.

Certainly, the struggle between Arcadia and destiny is not dead in California writing. The dream of an earthly paradise of health and natural beauty hovers in the background of books by writers as various as Wallace Stegner, Maxine Hong Kingston, James D. Houston, Dorothy Bryant, Jack Kerouac, Diane Johnson, and Richard Brautigan, just as the violent subversion or destruction of the dream often occupies the foreground. It is hard not to dream such dreams in California on the perfectly warm and tranquil October days that prevail up and down the coast, when the first rains have washed the air to an intoxicating clarity that makes every leaf and grain of sand sparkle.

FARM KNOLL AT CONTRA COSTA, 1970

PHOTOGRAPHER'S NOTES BY MORLEY BAER

IT WAS ABOUT THIRTY YEARS AGO that I first began to accumulate detailed notes (gradually to become photographs) comparing the California coast with various parts of the eastern seaboard, which I enjoyed as a youngster. The comparisons were tenuous. A sunny afternoon spent immersed in foam and sandstone on the south shore of Point Lobos was overwhelming. A similar afternoon spent climbing around on the boulders above the beach at Ogunquit was a poor comparison. Similarly, the never-ending flat and open sands of Trinidad Beach easily outstripped a first-time-ever swim on The Cape.

Ruminations such as these left me with the certainty that the California shoreline was a better place to live—better because its diversity was greater, its sands and stones rougher, its waters more turbulent (and fifty degrees colder), its skies a deeper blue, and its atmosphere more stimulating than anything I remembered from that old east coast of my childhood. It seemed to me a greater sense of space prevailed here facing the Pacific, a space uncluttered by the usual residue of man. Surely, out of such space a beneficent solitude could be drawn—just what was needed for the cogitation, contemplation, and other somewhat undefinable states required for the making of great photographs.

Though I was to find the stuff of which photographs could be made in every part of California I visited (this book contains the evidence), it was the coast that first drew me and continues to be the principal subject of my landscape work. It was the turmoil of land meeting sea that started me on my present course. I found myself standing one day against the back of the car looking almost straight down into the brilliant, foamy surf breaking against the bottom of Devil's Slide. It struck me then—and the image continues to be a source of photographs yet to be taken—that I was being enraptured by what is probably the most ferocious natural activity on the California coast. Here was a place where natural forces wage continual battle. I was to see comparable battles at Point Cabrillo and Point Conception, along the Sur Coast and the Sonoma shoreline, and on the Mendocino headlands—here on the California coast is epitomized the ultimate argument between land and sea. Nowhere else is the conflict more impressive. Nowhere else are the natural fundaments at the edge of a continent arrayed in such magnificent opposition.

How does one convey this photographically? Is there more here at work than just physical nature? And what of the paradox that in so profound a struggle there is no victor, no vanquished? Natural forces in action are seldom explained by photographs of their components; and, besides, photographs are more often metaphor than expla-

151

nation. After living for some years on the California coast, and always *with* the California coast, I developed a sense that it was not only forces *out there* that were the subjects of photographs, but also the forces *in here*; not only the wondrous materials of the world, but also the emotional apparatus that acts in response. It is the response of mind and heart that forges links with place.

I have lived and worked for more than thirty-five years on the California coast. My connection with this place is as firm as the rock that punctuates its edge. I am still in awe of the forces displayed in contest here and can still stand on the rocky ledge at Point Lobos called "the slot," breathe deeply of the salt air, and feel the place in my bones. This wilder shore, which shapes all life here, is made of many parts, reaching far inland to touch other places in the state. *The Wilder Shore* as a photographic statement comes, then, as much from my mind and heart as from physical California, the product of that inexplicable response of person to place. It is only a hint of the appreciation I feel for the sublime experience of living in a place I love.

Except for a few instances in which conditions dictated the use of 35mm equipment, all photographs in *The Wilder Shore* were made with an eight-by-ten Ansco View Camera, now about fifty years old. Age has made its bellows more flexible, worn its track, and required a few extra wood screws to hold its parts securely, but all this contributes nothing to the facility of using it. Only familiarity can do that. Although the eye of the photographer is a composite of character, opportunity, mindset, and a hundred other factors, whatever I have learned about seeing is at least in part because of my habitual use of this camera since 1947.

With a series of lenses, stepping up from very short (121mm) to fairly long (30-inch), film holders, and accessories, it is a tactical problem to go very far from the car. I usually pack the camera, already fastened to the large wooden tripod, over one shoulder and balance that weight by carrying in my other hand a fitted aluminum box that holds lenses, film holders, and accessories.

This is in no way a recommendation of large format equipment for anyone else working in the field. In the late thirties when I first began photographing seriously, no other camera could give me the precision, directness, and clarity that was possible with eight-by-ten negatives and the resultant contact prints. This is not true today. But neither my habits of seeing, nor my ways of working have kept pace with technological "progress." Individual style comes, no doubt, from one's method of working —seeing clearly, then using equipment, materials, and accessories in a pattern to produce a consistent body of work. The body of work in this book is in part the product of habits associated with the use of my now-elderly view camera.

Super XX is the only black-and-white film I have used for many years. I find its long scale, after development in ABC Pyro, to be a firm base for the emphasis on middle tones, which I particularly desire in photographs. It is this "silvery" part of a black-and-white photograph that gives me personal satisfaction. Super XX, with proper changes in development times, also makes possible contraction or expansion of brightness values, an important element in photographs of natural scenes. Rarely can one photograph a landscape "as is." Often extreme exaggeration is called for if the result is to be compelling.

For color reproduction I have chosen to work with eight-by-ten Professional Ektachrome. The film is far more limiting in its range than, for instance, color negative material would be. Again, familiarity dictated the choice. The use of color negatives would have entailed, for a print or transparency from each piece of film, a well-exercised rapport with a darkroom assistant. Ektachrome made it possible for me to depend upon standard processing procedures, requiring no additional judgment from another person. All transparencies were exposed at double the rated film speed. Processing was altered accordingly.

Working on the shoreline with color materials, one recognizes a preponderance of cyan in everything. (Even a casual observer might say that the atmosphere looks as if it is loaded with blue.) By itself color film cannot compensate for this natural color imbalance. I usually use one of the Series 81 filters to alter the light passing through the camera and to make the general atmosphere of a coastal scene more acceptable.

Wherever the range of brightness values allowed me to do so, I exposed longer than what is considered normal. I believe that California's natural forms are nothing like the oily, heavy, oversaturated color I often see printed in magazines and books. Color reproduction has disturbed me for many years because of the constant emphasis on color at the expense of other elements. I found, while working on this book, that slight and careful overexposure of Ektachrome helped to reduce, where I chose to do so, color saturation and to allow elements of form to take more importance. I persist in believing that this is not Kodachrome California, that our natural scene has more form and spirit than can usually be expressed with strong emphasis on color alone.

It may be helpful for other photographers to know that the color reproductions in this book were made directly from the in-camera transparencies, not from reflective prints. Both color and black-and-white subjects were transferred to lithographic materials by the laser scanner. All black-and-white subjects were scanned and printed as duotones in two black inks.

NOTES

156

157

158

BIBLIOGRAPHY

Austin, Mary. *The Land of Little Rain*. Gloucester, Mass.: Peter Smith, 1969.

Bierce, Ambrose. *Can Such Things Be?* New York: A & C Boni, 1909.

Chandler, Raymond. *The Raymond Chandler Omnibus: Four Famous Classics*. New York: Alfred A. Knopf, 1964.

Dana, Richard Henry. *Two Years Before the Mast*. Harvard Classics Edition. New York: P. F. Collier & Son, 1968.

Didion, Joan. *Slouching Towards Bethlehem*. New York: Farrar, Straus & Giroux, 1968.

————. *The White Album*. New York: Simon & Schuster, 1979.

Everson, William. *Archetype West: The Pacific Coast as a Literary Region*. Berkeley: Oyez, 1976.

Harte, Bret. *The Writings of Bret Harte*. Riverside Edition. Boston: Houghton Mifflin, 1920.

Jackson, Helen Hunt. *Ramona: A Story*. Boston: Little, Brown & Co., 1939.

Jeffers, Robinson. *The Double Axe and Other Poems*. New York: Liveright, 1977.

————. *Not Man Apart: Lines from Robinson Jeffers*. San Francisco: Sierra Club Books, 1965.

————. *The Selected Poetry of Robinson Jeffers*. Modern Library Edition. New York: Random House, 1937.

London, Jack. *The Sea Wolf*. New York: Macmillan, 1904.

————. *The Valley of the Moon*. Santa Barbara: Peregrine Smith Inc., 1975.

Miller, Henry. *Big Sur and the Oranges of Hieronymus Bosch*. New York: New Directions, 1957.

Muir, John. *John of the Mountains: The Unpublished Journals of John Muir*. Edited by Linnie Marsh Wolf. Madison, Wis.: University of Wisconsin Press, 1979.

————. *The Mountains of California*. Garden City, New York: Doubleday & Co., 1961.

————. *My First Summer in the Sierra*. Boston: Houghton Mifflin, 1916.

————. *The Yosemite*. Garden City, New York: Doubleday & Co., 1962.

Norris, Frank. *McTeague: A Story of San Francisco*. New York: The New American Library, 1964.

————. *The Octopus: A Story of California*. New York: A. Wessels Company, 1906.

Powell, Lawrence Clark. *California Classics*. Los Angeles: Ward Ritchie Press, 1971.

Ricketts, Edward Flanders, and Calvin, Jack. *Between Pacific Tides*. Stanford: Stanford University Press, 1948.

Roper, Robert. *On Spider Creek*. New York: Simon & Schuster, 1978.

Snyder, Gary. *The Back Country*. New York: New Directions, 1968.

————. *The Old Ways: Six Essays*. San Francisco: City Lights Books, 1977.

Starr, Kevin. *Americans and the California Dream*. New York: Oxford University Press, 1973.

Steinbeck, John. *Cannery Row*. New York: Bantam Books, 1972.

————. *The Grapes of Wrath*. Middlesex, England: Penguin Books, 1970.

————. *The Long Valley*. New York: Bantam Books, 1970.

————. *To a God Unknown*. New York: Bantam Books, 1960.

Stevenson, Robert Louis. *The Silverado Squatters*. Vailima Edition. New York: P. F. Collier & Son, 1912.

Twain, Mark. *Roughing It*. Authorized Uniform Edition. New York: Harper and Brothers, 1899.

INDEX

References to the photographs are in italic type.